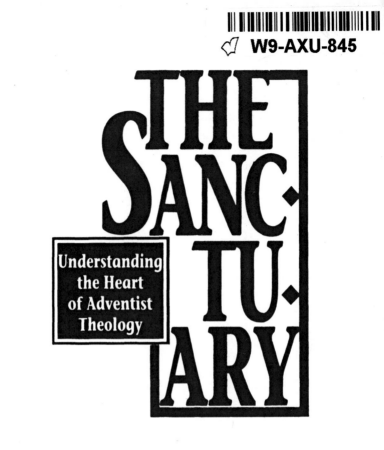

THE SANC·TU·ARY

Understanding the Heart of Adventist Theology

THE SANCTUARY

Understanding the Heart of Adventist Theology

ROY ADAMS

REVIEW AND HERALD® PUBLISHING ASSOCIATION
HAGERSTOWN, MD 21740

The author assumes full responsibility for the accuracy of all facts and quotations
as cited in this book.

Scripture quotations marked NASB are from the *New American Standard Bible*, © The
Lockman Foundation 1960, 1962, 1963, 1968, 1971, 1972, 1973, 1975, 1977.

Bible texts credited to Phillips are from J. B. Phillips: *The New Testament in Modern English*,
Revised Edition. © J. B. Phillips 1958, 1960, 1972. Used by permission of Macmillan
Publishing Co., Inc.

Bible texts credited to RSV are from the Revised Standard Version of the Bible, copyright ©
1946, 1952, 1971, by the Division of Christian Education of the National Council of the
Churches of Christ in the U.S.A. Used by permission.

This book was
Edited by Richard W. Coffen
Designed by Bill Kirstein
Cover design by Helcio Deslandes
Typeset: 11/12 Cheltenham Nova

PRINTED IN U.S.A.

98 97 96 95 94 93   10 9 8 7 6 5 4 3 2 1

Library of Congress Cataloging in Publication Data
Adams, Roy, 1941-
    The sanctuary: understanding the heart of Adventist theology /
Roy Adams.
        p.   cm.
    1. Sanctuary doctrine (Seventh-day Adventists) 2. Seventh-day
Adventists—Doctrines. 3. Adventists—Doctrines. I. Title.
BX6154.A562   1993
230'.6732—dc20   92-14249
                                                     CIP

ISBN 0-8280-0656-3

Contents

Preface

After finishing my doctoral dissertation on the doctrine of the sanctuary as taught by Seventh-day Adventists, I received a request from an editor of Southern Publishing Association in Nashville, Tennessee, to popularize the work for general Adventist readership. With all good intentions I agreed, but the years fled by, and I never completed work on the manuscript. The pressure of the immediate held the day.

The book you now hold in your hand indicates that somewhere along the way, I managed to resist that pressure of the immediate long enough to prepare a book-length manuscript dealing with the sublime theme before us. However, it is not—as originally intended—a popularization of my dissertation. That work has now been published on its own in the Andrews University Seminary Doctoral Dissertation Series.* Rather, the present book has grown out of notes I made as I wrote that dissertation, jottings of ideas that I could not include in it. These random scribblings eventually developed into class lectures, sermons, presentations at pastors' meetings, and now into this book.

Unlike my dissertation, which I commenced and completed *before* the crisis over the doctrine of the sanctuary in the Adventist Church broke in the early 1980s (and therefore was not written as a response to it), this book has been written with that challenge in mind. I could not pretend to write it as if that development had never happened.

However, the real impetus for this effort is much broader than that event. It is an intensification of the original drive that sparked my dissertation on the sanctuary in the first place: a concern to evaluate *for myself* the integrity of this tenet of Adventist faith. The wisecracks, the snickering, the innuendos, the skeleton-in-the-closet mentality that I'd encountered in some quarters within the church vis-à-vis the sanctuary doctrine had stung me. I'd also been sobered by the hostile press the doctrine had received by those not of our faith.

Since these motivations are real, the reader will see evidence of them in the work. I hope it will also become clear that I am interested in the sanctuary theme *for its own sake!* For some reason deep down within, I find myself completely fascinated with this concept of a heavenly sanctuary, and I have always approached its study with a sense of awe and wonder.

This being the case, I consider the present book a personal testimony shared for the simple purpose of clarifying my own position on certain key areas of the subject. If it helps to affirm the faith of those who already accept the doctrine, this will be reward enough. If it also succeeds in confirming the faith of those who are wavering, that would be a most welcome bonus. I even have the temerity to hope that perhaps in one or two cases it may stimulate the interest of perfect strangers in the doctrine or create respect for the teaching in minds that once opposed or ridiculed it. All these extras I leave entirely up to Providence. Nonetheless, they did influence somewhat the way I have presented the case.

I would like to remember with gratitude my students at our seminary in the Philippines, against whom I bounced off many of the ideas I express here and whose questions and comments further stimulated my interest in this subject.

In addition, and in particular, I am grateful to four of my former teachers: William Johnsson, William Shea, Robert Johnston, and Raoul Dederen, who took time from their horrendously busy schedules to read the original manuscript and offer invaluable suggestions. I have always felt at liberty—since classroom days when, with tired fingers, I wrote down their every word—to borrow from my teachers without attribution, and I have done so in this work perhaps even more than I know. But all blunders are my own.

A word of thanks is also in order to the secretaries who typed and retyped the manuscripts during the long period of gestation:

Ruby Orate and Puring Raqui, from our seminary in the Philippines, and Nicole Bolder, my present secretary. But the maddening share of the work was done by Chitra Barnabas, my former secretary, who painstakingly transcribed hours and hours of tape, as I revised earlier written drafts beyond legibility.

The editorial staff at the Review and Herald Publishing Association manages to treat you as if yours were the only manuscript to claim their attention. I want to thank them—and, in particular, Richard Coffen, who saw the manuscript through the final editing process and has made many valuable suggestions.

I also thank my wife, Celia, and my children, Dwayne and Kim, for allowing me to remain in "exile" with this work on so many occasions when I should have been with them.

Finally, though foremost, my deepest gratitude flows to the Lord, whose grace marvelously sustained me throughout the project.

---

* Roy Adams, *The Sanctuary Doctrine: Three Approaches in the Seventh-day Adventist Church* (Berrien Springs, Mich.: Andrews University Press, 1981). Hereinafter referred to as *The Sanctuary Doctrine*.

Introduction

Understandably some within the church will always be uncomfortable with the idea of change when it comes to matters of doctrine. One reason for this is that some see the church as having the truth, the whole truth, and nothing but the truth.

TRUTH EVER EXPANDING

I find it interesting and significant, however, that Ellen G. White, one of the staunchest among us and one who, as we believe, was enlightened by the prophetic gift, did not take that position.

"There is no excuse for anyone in taking the position that there is no more truth to be revealed, and that all our expositions of Scripture are without an error. The fact that certain doctrines have been held as truth for many years by our people is not a proof that our ideas are infallible. Age will not make error into truth, and truth can afford to be fair. No doctrine will lose anything by close investigation." [1]

I think the fundamental rationale for the development of doctrine is our humanity, limitedness, and shortsightedness. We do not perceive at any one time all that God wants to say to us. That is why Jesus said to His followers on the eve of His death: "I have yet many things to say to you, but you cannot bear them now" (John 16:12, RSV).

It seems that at crucial points in history the church becomes afflicted with something in the nature of spiritual myopia, making it difficult to see ahead, difficult to appreciate the full counsel that God wishes to give. The church's immediate context—whether social, political, religious, or ideological—limits it and puts blinders on its eyes.

One of those times was the eve of the cross, when the disciples remained confused notwithstanding Christ's best efforts to enlighten them. Another was the time of the Reformation, when even giants like Martin Luther could not see beyond some of the walls that tradition had built up over the centuries. A third occasion was 1844—a time of enormous theological insights, great expectation, and heightened spiritual fervor, but a time that was to witness one of the most crushing disappointments in the history of the church. The Millerites, despite the correctness of their position on many counts, nevertheless became afflicted with a theological mental block, so to speak, that made it difficult for them to appreciate certain elementary biblical truths. In particular, they failed to reckon with Jesus' clear statement that no one knows the day and hour of His coming, "not even the angels of heaven, nor the Son, but the Father only" (Matt. 24:36, RSV).

And it was in 1844, one of those difficult periods, that God came to some of His disappointed, broken, discouraged people with the marvelous truth of the sanctuary. How we could expect them to have seen everything He wanted to show them through their disappointment and tear-filled eyes has always escaped me. I have always believed that God gave them just as much as they were able to grasp in their moment of defeat, enough to surmount the predicament that faced them.

The doctrine of the sanctuary is one of the most sensitive areas of Adventist faith, and no cautious Adventist theologian rushes into it without pause. My venture into this field, therefore, is deliberate and calculated, founded on the belief that our historic nervousness about this point is outdated and unwarranted. I have a sense that we have now come far enough for an honest and, so far as we can achieve it, candid reflection on this important theme.

Considerable history now lies behind us, and part of that history shows that our thinking on the sanctuary doctrine has not been frozen. Of particular interest to me in this connection is the evident modification of our position on the atonement, a central facet of the sanctuary theme.

In 1905 Albion Fox Ballenger[2] fell under the wrath of Adventist Church leaders for teaching, among other things, that the atonement was finished at the cross.[3] His trial was held in a small building in Takoma Park, Maryland, at the site of the church's General Conference session that year. Milian Lauritz Andreasen,[4] then a young unordained minister, tells how he and fellow minister L. H. Christian took turns standing on each other's shoulders so as to eavesdrop on the proceedings of that predawn inquiry.[5] Under the light of day, as other meetings of the session proceeded, Andreasen took time to canvass the views of the embattled pariah. With much time on his hands—so few of the more experienced brethren had time for him—Ballenger shared freely.[6]

The irony of the situation was to come some 50 years later when Andreasen found himself at serious loggerheads with church leaders over the very question of the atonement—among others. This time, curiously, it was the church that defended the view of a finished atonement at the cross, with Andreasen digging in his heels for an unfinished atonement, the very position church leaders were championing in 1905.[7]

To conclude from this that the church's position on the sanctuary (or on other points of doctrine) is fluid would, of course, be completely unwarranted. Nor does it follow that the church will eventually come around to any deviant position, regardless of the merits of the case. What it shows, rather, is that the church is not closed and that, however slowly, it does move eventually in the direction the Spirit is leading.

We should, therefore, not approach the doctrine of the sanctuary as if the church has learned nothing new since our pioneers fell asleep. All human existence experiences change, and with the change of experience comes also a change in our perception of (unchanging) truth. Theology, therefore, is never static. The path of the righteous is like the light of dawn that looms ever brighter unto the perfect day (Prov. 4:18). We are standing on the shoulders of our pioneers, and we ought to be able to see a little farther than they did. We dishonor their intrepid legacy if we don't.

In admitting, however, that we stand upon their shoulders, we imply as a matter of course that they themselves stood on a solid platform. So those who expect the shaking of the pillars in these pages will probably be disappointed. If the foundation is solid, then nothing I say here can shake it.

I think the key to understanding what I am about is the word "reflections." It suggests that I do not see myself as providing, in any sense, a definitive articulation (or even rearticulation) of the Adventist position on the sanctuary. The subject is so vast that it would take the combined effort of many people to explore its full dimensions. I can only hope that readers will accept this effort as merely one student's attempt, within his own contemporary setting, to understand a few chapters of the most marvelous truth in sacred Scripture, the salvation God has provided in Jesus Christ—for that's what the doctrine of the sanctuary is all about.

KEEPING IT SIMPLE

It has not been my aim to write a scholarly tome, and I have not done so. I wanted to write a book that Adventists untrained in theology can pick up and follow without much difficulty. I wanted a book that would not appear forbidding to the average reader because of an abundance of scholarly jargon and technical references.

Even so, I found it impossible to proceed without a minimum of such terms and references. There were certain areas in which technicalities and reference materials could not be completely avoided without affecting credibility. I can only hope that, where used, they enhance the usefulness of the book.

No one should expect to agree with me on every point. That would be impossible and unnecessary. The book will have achieved its goal if, notwithstanding the multitude of details and even areas of disagreement along the way, the reader can join me in a peek or two through the open gates of heaven into the throne room of the universe, the nerve center of our redemption. My prayer is that through this feeble effort many readers may come to know a deeper appreciation for the sublime truth of the sanctuary and a fuller surrender to the One who occupies its shining center.

---

[1] Ellen G. White, *Counsels to Writers and Editors* (Nashville: Southern Pub. Assn., 1946), p. 35.

[2] Albion Ballenger (1861-1921) served the church in the capacity of teacher, pastor, and evangelist in the 1890s and until 1905. See Adams, *The Sanctuary Doctrine*, pp. 11, 12.

[3] *Ibid.*, pp. 121-123, 150-152.

[4] Milian L. Andreasen (1876-1962) served the church for some five decades as an administrator and educator.

[5] *Ibid.*, p. 165, n. 2. The inquiry took place in the predawn hours, probably for privacy or maybe in order not to get in a tight session agenda.

[6] *Ibid.*, n. 3.

[7] *Ibid.*, pp. 212-219.

CHAPTER 1

Metaphors of Redemption and Restoration:

KEEPING CALVARY IN CONSTANT VIEW

Not long after the Creation—no one knows the exact time—our first parents fell into sin. The sad story of their dismissal from the Garden of Eden is recorded in Genesis 3:22-24: "The Lord God said, 'Behold, the man has become like one of us, knowing good and evil; and now, lest he put forth his hand and take also of the tree of life, and eat, and live for ever'—therefore, the Lord God sent him forth from the garden of Eden, to till the ground from which he was taken. He drove out the man; and at the east of the garden of Eden He placed the cherubim, and a flaming sword which turned every way, to guard the way to the tree of life" (RSV).

In the wake of this terrible crisis, God's first concern was for human restoration and the eternal security of the universe. The death of a member of the Godhead—a contingency already determined in the foreknowledge and council of God (see Rev. 13:8)—was the only means to that end.

To secure human participation and cooperation in this supreme endeavor, God moved quickly to inform our first parents of the plan. At the same time, He put in place a teaching device to keep it perpetually before their attention and that of succeeding generations.

We find cryptic evidence of these divine initiatives in the book of Genesis. Speaking to the serpent, evidently in the hearing of the ancient couple, God said: "I will put enmity between you and the woman, and between your seed and her seed; he shall bruise your head, and you shall bruise his heel" (Gen. 3:15, RSV). Historically, this passage has been interpreted as a forecast of the coming of Messiah and of the divine victory over the forces of evil. So conceived, it was to our first parents a promise of salvation and restoration providing strong incentives for the struggle against the evil that lay ahead of them.

In order to keep ever before their memory the plan of redemption and the certainty of ultimate victory already implicit in the *protoevangelium*[2] of Genesis 3:15, God instituted a program of blood sacrifice, the first hint of which appears in the fourth chapter of Genesis in a passage designed to highlight the theological significance of the symbolism.

"In the course of time Cain brought to the Lord an offering of the fruit of the ground, and Abel brought of the firstlings of his flock and of their fat portions. And the Lord had regard for Abel and his offering, but for Cain and his offering he had no regard" (Gen. 4:3-5, RSV).

From what at its first inception at least must have been a most painful and excruciating exercise, God intended that His people should learn at least three important things: (1) that sin costs, (2) that sin brings death, and (3) that He will Himself provide a substitute for us (cf. Gen. 22:8).

As performed during the first 2,500 years or so of human history—or up to the time of the Exodus—this practice of blood sacrifice possibly consisted of the simple slaying of the innocent animal victim, the shedding of its blood, and the offering of its body as a burnt sacrifice. The evidence for this claim is not quite as compelling as one would wish. The first clear scripture for the actual offering up of a burnt sacrifice comes at the end of the Flood. The record says that Noah offered "burnt offerings" (Gen. 8:20), evidently in gratitude for God's protection during the Deluge.

The same passage in Genesis mentions the building of an altar. The Hebrew word for altar is *mizbeach*. It comes from *zabach*, "to slaughter." This probably means that whenever we hear about altar-building, we are to assume the slaughter of a sacrificial animal victim and the giving of its body in burnt offering, for that is what it would have meant to the Hebrew mind. If this is so, then we have several instances of blood sacrifice on the part of the patriarchs, spanning several generations: Abraham (Gen. 12:7, 8); Isaac (Gen. 26:24, 25); Jacob (Gen. 35:7); and Moses (Ex. 17:15).

Perhaps the most explicit evidence of blood sacrifice since the post-Flood offerings by Noah and his family is that connected with the test of Abraham. You recall that Abraham, having passed the divine test of obedience, found a ram caught in a thicket and it became the victim-substitute (Gen. 22:7, 13). The idea of animal sacrifice is also evident in Moses' insistence before Pharaoh that their flocks and herds leave Egypt with the Israelites, so that they might "have sacrifices and burnt offerings, that we may sacrifice to the Lord our God" (Ex. 10:25, 26, RSV).

If all this is correct, then we have here what might be considered fundamental to the whole sacrificial system: *the simple slaying of the animal victim, the spilling of its blood, and the offering of its body as a burnt sacrifice.* It is important to keep this in mind so we do not become overly distracted by later elaborations.

NEW DEVELOPMENTS

When the Israelites came to Mount Sinai in their journey from Egypt, God gave new instructions for an elaborate sacrificial system centered on a formal priesthood and the establishment of what we know today as the tabernacle and its services. The interpretation of the ceremonies and symbols involved in this system and their application for today have given rise to considerable theological discussion (not to say controversy) within the Adventist Church. They have also raised suspicion and questions in the minds of non-Adventist observers. I intend to take up some of those concerns shortly.

But perhaps we ought first to set the whole issue in proper perspective by a brief assessment of the reasons for the establishment of the more structured sacrificial system at Sinai. I offer three.

1. *To provide tangible evidence of the divine presence.* Communing with Moses on Mount Sinai, God said to him: "And let them make me a sanctuary; that I may dwell among them" (Ex. 25:8). In this passage we have, as a matter of fact, the only clear, explicit reason for the erection of the tabernacle and the inauguration of its services. In Eden God had held unimpaired, face-to-face communication with our first parents. With the inception of sin, the experience of open communion came to an end, and a perception of distance—on humanity's part—arose.

By the time of the Egyptian experience (and, indeed, *because* of that experience), this perception of distance had grown acute. We sense this in the reaction of the people as Moses and Aaron met with them. "Then Moses and Aaron went and gathered together all the elders of the people of Israel. And Aaron spoke all the words which the Lord had spoken to Moses, and did the signs in the sight of the people. And the people believed; *and when they heard that the Lord had visited the people of Israel* and that he had seen their affliction, they bowed their heads and worshiped" (Ex. 4:29-31, RSV).

Evidently they were moved by the revelation that the One who appeared so far away from them, the One whom they thought had abandoned them to abject servitude and a meaningless destiny, was indeed concerned about them. He had come—to use the expression in the passage above—to "visit" them.

In the establishment of the tabernacle, then, God wanted His people to know that His presence among them was not to be regarded as a temporary "visit" occasioned by their plight. Rather,

He had come among them to stay. The Hebrew word used in Exodus 25:8, *shakan* (to dwell), connotes permanent residency in a community. The community may, indeed, move from one locality to another, but God's residency in it, His solidarity with it, and His presence within it would remain unbroken. "Let them make me a sanctuary; that I may dwell [permanently] among them."

So as the tabernacle was erected, a mysterious cloud came over it, "and the glory of the Lord filled" it. And "throughout all their journeys the cloud of the Lord was upon the tabernacle by day, and fire was in it by night, in the sight of all . . . Israel" (Ex. 40:34, 38, RSV).

Deprived of regular religious instruction through hundreds of years of servitude in Egypt, the Israelites had virtually lost contact with the sacred traditions of their ancestors. Their ability to conceptualize divine realities was at an all-time low—witness, for example, their demand for visible gods when Moses delayed on Mount Sinai (Ex. 32:1). They needed this tangible evidence of divine presence, and God met them where they were by providing the sanctuary service.

To view the wilderness encampment from high ground was to see the tabernacle in the center, surrounded on all four sides by the tents of Israel (see diagram next page).

Immediately surrounding the tabernacle on all four sides were the Levites (Num. 1:50, 53). Of these Levites, only the priestly class (Aaron and his sons) together with Moses were to occupy the eastern side of the entrance into the court and tabernacle. "And those to encamp before the tabernacle on the east, before the tent of meeting toward the sunrise, were Moses and Aaron and his sons, having charge of the rites within the sanctuary" (Num. 3:38, RSV; cf. Ex. 27:9-16).

On each of the four sides, beyond the dwelling of the Levites, were three of the other tribes of Israel, the most prominent of the three giving its name to that particular segment of the camp. On the east, for example, was the "camp of Judah," composed of Judah,

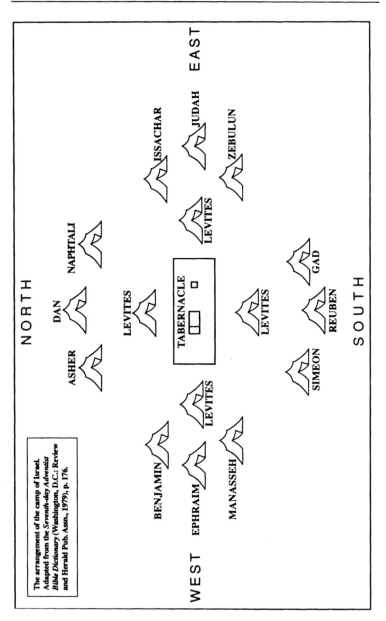

The arrangement of the camp of Israel. Adapted from the *Seventh-day Adventist Bible Dictionary* (Washington, D.C.: Review and Herald Pub. Assn., 1979), p. 176.

Issachar, and Zebulun. On the south was the camp of Reuben, composed of Reuben, Simeon, and Gad; etc. (Num. 2).[3] The arrangement thus represented a vivid portrayal of the sanctuary as the symbol of divine presence in the midst of Israel.

In the process of showing God's presence among His people, this encampment of the tabernacle in the midst of Israel highlighted two other important theological truths.

i. The arrangement was a proleptic "statement" regarding the nature and coming of Messiah. In other words, it portrayed in anticipation the Incarnation. "And they shall call His name Immanuel," says Matthew's Gospel, "which translated means, 'God with us' " (Matt. 1:23, NASB). That, precisely, was what the sanctuary meant to Israel.

John, in what appears to be an even clearer allusion to the ancient tabernacle arrangement, declared: "The Word became flesh and dwelt [literally, "tabernacled"] among us" (John 1:14, RSV). And as if to recall the glory of God settling over the wilderness tabernacle in full view of the surrounding encampment, he added: "And we beheld His glory" (NASB).

The wilderness encampment thus provided a beautiful picture of the coming of Messiah.

ii. The tabernacle encampment emphasized two important aspects of deity: *immanence* and *transcendence.*

The reason for the Levite ring around the tabernacle is expressly stated in the text: "So when the tabernacle is to set out, the Levites shall take it down; and when the tabernacle encamps, the Levites shall set it up. *But the layman who comes near shall be put to death.* . . . But the Levites shall camp around the tabernacle . . . *that there may be no wrath on the congregation of the sons of Israel"* (Num. 1:51-53, NASB). The same warning is repeated in chapter 3, verse 38.

Immanence refers to the nearness, the presence, or the indwelling of God in His creation. The location of the tabernacle in midcamp was meant to underline this aspect of God. He comes near to His people. He takes up permanent residence in their midst. What a joy—and what sense of security—must have come from having God so very close!

Transcendence, on the other hand, refers to God's "otherness," God's unapproachableness, His apartness or distance from us. Thus the restrictions placed upon freedom of access to the tabernacle area by the "buffer zone" of Levites and priests suggested that although tabernacled amid His people, God was still the transcendent, unapproachable One of awful holiness and majesty—the *Deus absconditus*, as Luther was fond of saying.[4]

This arrangement suggested the need for a middleman, a mediator. And whereas limited access was provided through the Levitical priests, we now know that this all pointed forward to a heavenly Priest-Mediator, who was to open a door of unlimited access to the throne of the living God. In Christ every barrier is broken down, so that the author of Hebrews could call upon us to "draw near" with "confidence" to the throne of grace in full assurance (Heb. 4:16, RSV).

2. *To provide for a centralized system of worship.* Israelite society having now become more complex and diversified, there was the need for a centralized system of worship as a preventive against abuse and idolatry.

During the patriarchal period God was dealing primarily with single families. The structure needed to be kept simple, and it was. Abraham and the other patriarchs, as "priest" of the family, could lead out in presenting the required sacrifices. But now Israel had grown into a large and complex nation composed of thousands of individual family units, making the ancient system inadequate. It would not be appropriate to erect thousands of altars in every place for presenting individual family offerings and sacrifices. The potential for abuse and distortion would be too great.

In order, therefore, to forestall this potential danger, God now issued directives for a centralized system of sacrificial worship directed no longer by patriarchal priests, but by a formally ordained and consecrated priestly tribe. Sacrifices would no longer be presented in every place, but rather in the one place specified. "But you shall seek the place which the Lord your God will choose out of all your tribes to put his name and make his habitation there; thither you shall go, and thither you shall bring your burnt offerings and your sacrifices. . . . Take heed that you do not offer your burnt offerings at every place that you see; but at the place which the Lord will choose in one of your tribes, there you shall offer your burnt offerings, and there you shall do all that I am commanding you" (Deut. 12:5-14, RSV).

This stipulation was all the more necessary because of the foreign influence among the people at this time. A sizable group of Egyptians (and possibly other nationalities as well) had left Egypt with the Israelites, perhaps in large part carried away by the signs and wonders they had witnessed. The Bible refers to these non-Israelites as a "mixed multitude" (Ex. 12:38; Num. 11:4). Some Bible versions even use the expression "rabble."[5]   They turned out to be a source of constant trouble for Moses and Israel, apparently instigating confusion and rebellion. This group, for example, initiated the rebellious demand for flesh food at Kibroth-hattaavah, a crisis that resulted in the death of thousands (see Num. 11:4-6, 18-20, 31-33).

Some evidence seems to suggest that elements of this "mixed multitude" sought also to foster a spirit of rebellion against the new centralized system of worship. Perhaps they capitalized on the disaffection of some heads of household who may have been reluctant to surrender their former rights and prerogatives to the sons of Aaron. The implication of Leviticus 17 is not only that some were offering sacrifices in places other than the sanctuary, but also that demonolatry (worship of demons) was involved (see Lev. 17:7).

Thus is it clear that certain abuses had indeed crept in among the people, making a centralized system of worship all the more necessary. Ellen G. White made this point in commenting on this new development. "The sacrificial system, committed to Adam, was also perverted by his descendants. Superstition, idolatry, cruelty, and licentiousness corrupted the simple and significant service that God had appointed. Through long intercourse with idolaters the people of Israel had mingled many heathen customs with their worship; therefore the Lord gave them at Sinai definite instruction concerning the sacrificial service." [6]

The centrality of the sanctuary for Israelite worship in succeeding centuries is evident in Solomon's prayer at the dedication of the Jerusalem Temple: "Yet have regard to the prayer of thy servant . . . that thy eyes may be open day and night *toward this house, the place where thou hast promised to set thy name*, that thou mayest hearken to the prayer which thy servant offers *toward this place. And hearken thou to the supplications of thy servant and of thy people Israel, when they pray toward this place*" (2 Chron. 6:19-21, RSV).

Thus the directional focus of Israel's national worship was a matter of fundamental importance, and we might even say that certain crucial details of the tabernacle structure were designed to reflect that sensitivity.

The door of the tabernacle, for example, was located on the eastern side. Therefore, as the worshiper looked in its direction, his back was turned toward the east. Evidently this was a symbolic repudiation of sun worship, which was widely practiced among ancient peoples. [7]

I think that this point emerges very clearly in the eighth chapter of Ezekiel. In that chapter the prophet is taken in vision to the Jerusalem Temple and shown the desecration of the sanctuary by the people of Israel. Four series of abominations are presented before him, ending with the most serious: "Then He brought me into the inner court of the Lord's house. And behold, at the entrance to the temple of the Lord, between the porch and the altar, were about twenty-five men with their backs to the temple of the Lord and their faces toward the east; and they were prostrating themselves eastward toward the sun" (Eze. 8:16, NASB).

To forestall this kind of development the entrance of the tabernacle/Temple was located on the eastern side. Moreover, in the case of the wilderness tabernacle, the tents of Moses, Aaron, and Aaron's sons were pitched permanently, so to speak, on the eastern side, looking toward the door, as if to represent a standing repudiation of sun worship on the part of the highest spiritual leaders of Israel.

Thus, it was God's purpose that the attention of all Israel should turn toward the sanctuary as the place of redemption, healing, and restoration. This is probably why Daniel, amid Babylonian idolatry, prayed with his windows open toward the Jerusalem Temple (Dan. 6:10), even as it lay in ruins.

3. *To provide additional details regarding the plan of salvation.* Here we begin to enter potentially controversial territory, and the reader will want to be most alert to the issues developing from this point on in the book.

It is true, as we have noted, that the fundamental point God wanted to communicate to humanity in regard to the plan of salvation was embodied in the simple act of slaying the innocent animal victim, spilling its blood, and offering its body in burnt sacrifice. But just as we observe a broadening revelation in respect to other biblical themes or concepts (for example, the Trinity, the Resurrection, the hereafter)—just so we may see in the establishment of the tabernacle with its elaborate ritual a divine purpose to supply additional information regarding God's saving activity in Jesus Christ.

We face, however, some interpretational problems here. The Old Testament provides very little explanation of the meaning of these services and rituals. We search in vain, for instance, for any explicit elaboration of the meaning of animal sacrifices beyond the (oft-repeated) purpose of making "an atonement" for the suppliant.[8] Other elaborate elements of the sacrificial system (such as *Yom Kippur* or Day of Atonement, with its "afflicting of the soul," its Sabbath rest, its Azazel or scapegoat ceremony) are stipulated without any real explanation whatsoever of their significance— either for that time or for the future.

Even the great feast of Passover seemed, from the Old Testament perspective, to look backward rather than forward. Indeed, modern Orthodox Jews when they observe it today still look back to the great event of the Exodus, just as their forefathers have done for thousands of years. They view the Passover, together with other ancient sacrificial rites, as simply fulfilling divine commands to offer them, lacking in any kind of typological significance.

Someone might say: Well, what about passages like Isaiah 53? Would that not have been clear enough to Israelites living in Isaiah's time? This is a fair question, but we must never forget that we today read such passages *after the fact*—through Christian eyes. Sometimes we need to put ourselves in the skin and mind of a person living six or seven centuries before the cross. How clear would the language of Isaiah 53 have been then?

I will never forget what happened one day in one of our seminary forums. A student asked our guest speaker, a rabbi, why Jews today do not see Isaiah 53 and Daniel 9 as prophecies of the Messiah. His reply was a classic. "It might be clear to you Christians," he said, "but it is not so clear to everybody that one is stupid not to see it."

I think he was correct. Isaiah 53 is not as unequivocal as we sometimes think. That's why the Ethiopian eunuch had trouble with it (see Acts 8:27-34). The lack of explicit biblical interpretation of these things is certainly an enigma to us.

Notwithstanding this silence, however, I would insist that one of the reasons for the establishment of the tabernacle and its services was precisely that of providing additional details of God's saving activity for humanity. It seems reasonable to assume that the ancient suppliant did not simply perform these rituals in complete ignorance of their meaning. And even though they did not always evidence the inquisitiveness of Greek (or Western) mentality, we would have to say that they did, at least, grasp the fact that these rituals pointed beyond themselves to some cosmic reality.

A rare hint of this—and I emphasize that it's only a hint—might be observed in Solomon's dedicatory prayer: "And hearken thou to the supplications of thy servant and of thy people Israel, when they pray toward this place; yea, *hear thou from heaven thy dwelling place; and when thou hearest, forgive.* If a man sins against his neighbor . . . and comes and swears his oath before thy altar in this house, *then hear thou from heaven . . ."* (2 Chron. 6:21-23, RSV).

This is significant when we remember that for the ancients prayer and temple pointed to sacrifice. They did not pray, as we do today, with nothing in their hands. They came with sacrifice, either actual or implied.[9] It is significant, then, that throughout his prayer Solomon makes *horizontal* reference to the Jerusalem Temple, then *vertical* reference to God's heavenly dwelling place. His hearers should have had no doubt about the real *source* of power and forgiveness, nor about the reality to which the earthly Temple and its sacrifices pointed.

But if Solomon's prayer is indeed a hint, it is a rare one. As a rule, there is virtually no substantial explanation of the cultic system in the ancient text. It keeps its knowledge to itself. Even the basic meaning of the sacrificial lamb, as we have already noted in connection with the Isaiah 53 passage, was held in silence until that reverent proclamation by the Baptist on the bank of Jordan: "Behold the Lamb of God, which taketh away the sin of the world" (John 1:29). With this terse announcement the curtain at last went up, and the silence was broken.

It brings to mind Jesus' statement regarding certain sayings or prophecies about Himself: "And now I have told you before it comes to pass, that when it comes to pass, you may believe" (John 14:29, NASB; cf. John 13:19; 16:4).

The Old Testament cultic system, then, is both parable and

prophecy. As parable it should not be expected, as the saying goes, "to walk on all fours." And as prophecy it needed fulfillment to disclose its meaning fully. When John made that immortal declaration by the Jordan at the beginning of Jesus' ministry, prophecy had met fulfillment. The One to whom the entire cultic system pointed had arrived. *In Him all the ancient metaphors of redemption and restoration found their meaning and fulfillment.*

So here and there throughout the New Testament we find a looking back to the ancient economy, with an application of its spiritual lessons for New Testament saints, "upon whom the end of the ages has come" (1 Cor. 10:11, RSV).

We now know the meaning of the "brazen" serpent in the wilderness. "As Moses lifted up the serpent in the wilderness, so must the Son of man be lifted up, that whoever believes in him may have eternal life" (John 3:14, 15, RSV).

We know the meaning of the rock in the desert. For they "all drank the same spiritual drink, for they were drinking from a spiritual rock which followed them; and the rock was Christ" (1 Cor. 10:4, NASB).

We know the meaning of Passover. "Christ our Passover . . . has been sacrificed" (1 Cor. 5:7, NASB).

And we know now why they burnt the sacrificial animals outside the camp of Israel. "The bodies of those animals . . . are burned outside the camp. Therefore Jesus also, that He might sanctify the people through His own blood, suffered outside the gate" (Heb. 13:11, 12, NASB).

But the definitive evidence that the ancient system pointed beyond itself to cosmic reality is found in the book of Hebrews, to which we will turn from time to time in subsequent chapters. Without the book of Hebrews we would still be virtually in the dark.

How much of all this did the ancient Israelites know? We shall never be sure this side of heaven, but we may hazard that a great many of them probably knew at least as much as Abraham, who, according to Jesus, perceived by faith through much less elaborate services the coming Messiah: "Your father Abraham rejoiced to see My day; and he saw it, and was glad" (John 8:56, NASB).

The fundamental point seems inescapable: God meant the ancient tabernacle/Temple and its rituals to be a teaching device — for Israel and for us.

---

[1] I use the term *metaphor* here in a broad sense to refer to figures, types, and symbols.

[2] This term means "first gospel" and refers to the initial proclamation of the good news by God Himself in Genesis 3:15 as it is traditionally understood.

[3] Note that the tribe of Levi was not listed in this camping enumeration since it already surrounded the sanctuary on all sides. To come up still with the important number 12, the tribe of Joseph was divided into Ephraim and Manasseh.

[4] The expression means "the hidden God" and is reminiscent of Isaiah 45:15: "Truly, thou art a God who hidest thyself" (RSV).

[5] See the RSV and NASB renderings of Numbers 11:4.

[6] Ellen G. White, *Patriarchs and Prophets* (Mountain View, Calif.: Pacific Press Pub. Assn., 1890), p. 364.

[7] I am indebted to A. F. Ballenger for this basic insight. See Adams, *The Sanctuary Doctrine*, pp. 279, 280. For evidence of the practice of sun worship among ancient Semitic peoples, see, for example, Deuteronomy 4:19; 17:3; 2 Kings 21:3, 5; *Interpreter's Dictionary of the Bible*, ed. George A. Buttrick (New York: Abingdon Press, 1962), vol. R-Z, pp. 462, 464.

[8] See Leviticus 1-4 for examples.

[9] I think that 1 Samuel 7:7-9 provides a good example of this.

CHAPTER 2

Activities and Paraphernalia of the Old Testament Sanctuary:

WHAT DID THEY SIGNIFY?

W hen I came to this point in my writing, I sensed the need to say something more about the meaning of certain aspects of the ancient tabernacle services and rituals. Yet these comments would not have flowed well with the drift of the previous chapter. The reader, I think, may elect to go on to the next chapter without sacrificing any vital links of the argument I am trying to build. Nonetheless, I feel impressed to include a few pages here on the theological significance of certain activities and things connected with the ancient service. I hope that the meanings we infer from the few selected examples might readily be seen as reasonable extrapolations[1] from the scriptural data.

As I already indicated in the preceding chapter, the Old Testament is almost completely silent on the meaning of practically all aspects of the ancient sanctuary economy. Not once does it explicitly inform us, for example, that the blood of the animal victim pointed to the blood of a crucified Messiah. For explicit comment on this most basic element of the sacrificial system, we must turn to the New Testament.

Notwithstanding the New Testament revelation, however, a

thousand other details remain shrouded in mystery, defying our native curiosity at every turn. A few scriptural hints break the otherwise total silence, and in these areas I wish to elaborate. In so doing, I will fall back from time to time on a few illuminating insights in the writings of Ellen G. White.

It will be seen at once that my purpose is not to be exhaustive but rather to illustrate the kind of sanctuary data on which we might focus with profit and the tentativeness that should characterize our interpretation. It should be clear that many of the items are too elusive for dogmatism.

THE SERVICES AND RITUALS

Every time I lectured on the subject of the tabernacle services and rituals during my days as a seminary teacher, I could expect to field questions regarding minute details of the sanctuary and its services. Some students were always fascinated by all the furniture, measurements, colors, and rituals. Perhaps there is a place for these minutiae, but I find myself naturally inclined to proceed in the opposite direction, especially as I have had numerous occasions to observe the speculative pitfalls that await those who indulge the appetite for finding hidden meanings in every detail of the ancient rituals.

As I move in the opposite direction, I try to note the significance only of the major aspects of the ritual as shown, for example, in the daily services.[2]

The daily services consisted of three main elements: the morning and evening burnt offering, the offering of incense on the golden altar located in the holy place, and the special offerings for personal sins (see Ex. 29:38-42; Num. 25:3-8; Ex. 30:6-8, 34-38; Lev. 4).

Every morning and evening a year-old lamb was burned on the altar in the courtyard. This piece of furniture was called, appropriately, the altar of *burnt offerings*. No explanation of this ritual can be found in the Old Testament. The statements in Isaiah (for instance, "like a lamb . . . led to the slaughter"—53:7, RSV) are really not explicit. Not until we come to the New Testament do we fully understand. As John sees the godly bearing of Jesus at the Jordan, he exclaimed in inspired wonder: "Behold, the Lamb of God, who takes away the sin of the world!" (John 1:29, RSV). And this one statement brings it all together for us.

Thus Ellen G. White could write that this daily offering of lambs in burnt sacrifice symbolized "the daily consecration of the nation to Jehovah, and their constant dependence upon the atoning blood of Christ." [3] This interpretation breathes credibility. It has not been lifted out of a hat or from someone's fertile imagination. And surely the offerings for personal sins would carry a similar meaning on the individual level.

She also comments on the meaning of the *incense* ritual, an aspect upon which the Bible is silent: "The incense, ascending with the prayers of Israel, represents the merits and intercession of Christ, His perfect righteousness, which through faith is imputed to His people, and which can alone make the worship of sinful beings acceptable to God." [4]

This helps us to understand the strong prohibition against duplicating the exact incense formula for any purpose except for use in the sanctuary service. "Whoever makes any like it to use as perfume shall be cut off from his people" (Ex. 30:37, 38, RSV). The concern was to ensure that such a formula would never be put to common use. I take the meaning for us today that we dare not attempt to duplicate the righteousness of Christ nor to invent our own way to approach God.

As regards the *shewbread*, again the Old Testament is silent, but the New Testament supplies a few significant hints. The most famous passage in this respect appears in John 6. A materialistically motivated search for Jesus by the recently fed multitude evokes the most extensive discourse on the symbolism of bread found anywhere in the Bible.

After frankly exposing their carnal motive for pursuing Him,

Jesus says to the people, "I am the bread of life" (verse 35).

They misunderstood Him. Again and again. But again and again, He presses home the figure: "I am the bread of life. Your fathers ate the manna in the wilderness, and they died. This is the bread which comes down out of heaven, so that one may eat of it and not die. I am the living bread that came down out of heaven; if any man eats of this bread, he shall live forever; and the bread also which I shall give for the life of the world is My flesh" (verses 48-51, NASB).

The Jews puzzled over the idea of eating Jesus' flesh. They were after food, all right, but they did not quite bargain for such a strange menu. Our Lord, for His part, made no apparent attempt to lessen their confusion. In fact, if indeed it was a genuine confusion, He, in effect, made it worse: "Truly, truly, I say to you, unless you eat the flesh of the son of Man and drink His blood, you have no life in yourselves. He who eats My flesh and drinks My blood has eternal life. . . . For My flesh is true food, and My blood is true drink" (verses 53-55, NASB).

Thus He proceeded, without letup, until He had made His crowning point: "He who eats this bread [pointing to His body, we would suppose] shall live forever" (verse 58, NASB).

Later, on the eve of His crucifixion in the solemn stillness of an upper room in Jerusalem, He would highlight the same symbolism: "And while they were eating, Jesus took some bread, and after a blessing, He broke it and gave it to the disciples, and said, 'Take, eat; this is My body' " (Matt. 26:26, NASB).

It is true that none of the passages just cited from John and Matthew harks back to the sanctuary shewbread. Jesus here was using manna typology, not shewbread typology. Yet I have the sense that the two are not unrelated. Ellen G. White interpreted the shewbread as "an acknowledgment of man's dependence upon God for both temporal and spiritual food . . . received only through the mediation of Christ." [5] Then, commenting on the famous Johannine passage just referred to, she said: "Both the manna and the shewbread pointed to Christ, the living Bread, who is ever in the presence of God for us." [6]

THE CUBICAL NATURE OF THE MOST HOLY PLACE

The Most Holy Place was a perfect cube. This was so in the wilderness tabernacle, in the Jerusalem Temple, in Ezekiel's ideal (or visionary) Temple, and, we may reasonably assume, in Zerubbabel's Temple also, though we have no record of its measurements. It might also be noted that the proportion between the sizes of the holy and the Most Holy places in the wilderness tabernacle was such that if the holy place was divided in half, two additional perfect cubes would have been created.

The constancy and persistency of this cubical characteristic in every manifestation of the tabernacle/Temple clearly means to point beyond itself. According to the *Interpreter's Dictionary of the Bible* (IDB), to cite one example, the number 3, as a recurring numeral in the tabernacle dimension, stands for divinity, and the perfect cube matches the perfection of the divine presence.[7] In other words, this source sees in the phenomenon of a perfect cube the perfection of the Trinity.

I consider this a valid interpretation of the phenomenon and would add to it the idea of the perfection of the divine dwelling place; for, after all, the Most Holy Place represented God's dwelling place on earth. G.R.H. Wright seems to allude to this point when he points to the square as "a very ancient conception" in temple architecture. Then he adds that "the square, or *a fortiori* a cube, has been associated with sacred architecture as a symbol of perfect space."[8]

And I observe that this cubical dimension finds an answer in the New Jerusalem, whose length, breadth, and height, we are told, are equal (Rev. 21:16)—meaning that the city is a perfect cube. The connection is significant when it is remembered that, like the Most Holy Place of the tabernacle/Temple, the New Jerusalem becomes God's dwelling place in the new cosmos among His people (verses 1-3, 22).

THE HIGH PRIEST'S DRESS

One of the most fascinating aspects of the ancient tabernacle/ Temple ritual was that of the high priest's clothing. The description given in Exodus 28:6-12 suggests an exquisitely gorgeous attire woven from the most costly material.

Outside the blue robe hung a shorter, sleeveless garment of gold, blue, purple, scarlet, and white—called the *ephod*. On its gold-embroidered shoulder pieces were set two onyx stones bearing the names of the 12 tribes of Israel. In this detail it was paralleled by the *breastplate* worn over the heart and constituted the most sacred part of the holy vestments.[9]

Those semiprecious gems of the breastplate, like the stones in the ephod, bore the names of the tribes of Israel, suggesting, says Ellen G. White in a beautiful commentary on the symbolism, that as Christ our Great High Priest pleads His blood before the Father, He bears upon His heart the name of every repentant, believing soul.[10]

Also forming part of the outfit were the *Urim* and *Thummim*, two large stones of great brilliancy through which God communicated His will to His people. Mrs. White says that in times of crisis, a halo of light encircled the Urim to indicate divine consent or approval, whereas a cloud overshadowing the Thummim at the left signaled divine disapproval.[11]

When we compare the high priest's dress with the description of the New Jerusalem in the book of Revelation, a number of intriguing conceptual connections surface.

The breastplate, for example, was designed in the shape of a square (Ex. 28:16), matching the description of the Holy City in Revelation 21:16: "And the city is laid out as a square" (NASB). Mounted on the breastplate, as noted above, was a variety of semiprecious stones arranged in four rows of three stones each. Like those in the shoulder pieces of the ephod, they were engraved with the names of the 12 tribes of Israel (Ex. 28:29). This feature answers to the inscriptions on the 12 gates of the City of God: "It had a great and high wall, with twelve gates, . . . and names were written on them, which are those of the twelve tribes of the sons of Israel" (Rev. 21:12, NASB).

In addition to these parallels, the stones on the breastplate bore a close affinity to those that form the 12 foundations of the New Jerusalem. Note the striking resemblance in the following two passages.

The Breastplate
"And you shall mount on it four rows of stones; the first row shall be a row of RUBY, TOPAZ and EMERALD; and the second row a TURQUOISE, a SAPPHIRE and a DIAMOND; and the third row a JACINTH, an AGATE and an AMETHYST; and the fourth row a BERYL and an ONYX and a JASPER; they shall be set in *gold* filigree" (Ex. 28:17-20, NASB).

The New Jerusalem
"The foundation stones of the city wall were adorned with every kind of precious stone. The first foundation stone was JASPER; the second, SAPPHIRE; the third, CHALCEDONY; the fourth, EMERALD; the fifth, SARDONYX; the sixth, SARDIUS; the seventh, CHRYSOLITE; the eighth, BERYL; the ninth, TOPAZ; the tenth, CHRYSOPRASE; the eleventh, JACINTH; the twelfth, AMETHYST" (Rev. 21:19, 20, NASB). "And the city was pure *gold*, like clear glass" (verse 18, NASB).

Anyone who has tried knows that these two lists of precious

stones cannot easily be reconciled. Indeed, as one commentator has noted with regard to the listing in Revelation, "even the most expert jeweler of today could not identify these twelve precious stones." Nor are we greatly helped, he says, by ancient literature, whose lists and descriptions of precious stones leave "so many unanswered questions." [12]

However, the point of our argument does not really turn on our ability to reconcile beyond doubt these two listings. It seems reasonable to suggest that the parallels already clearly established between other elements of the high priest's dress and the New Jerusalem—as well as numerous others that might be drawn— sufficiently demonstrate that, regardless of our present difficulty with identification, the list in Revelation 21 has been informed by the one in Exodus 28. We seem to find some kind of theological hint here. Says E. G. White, "The border [of the breastplate] was formed of a variety of precious stones, the same that form the twelve foundations of the City of God." [13]

Let me repeat that I understand the precarious nature of some of those comparisons. I am reminded that the book of Revelation echoes many parts of the Old Testament in presenting its own message. In Revelation, moreover, it is the names of the *apostles* that are on the foundation made up of these semiprecious stones (Rev. 21:14, 19-20) whereas the names of the *tribes* of Israel are on the gates, which are of pearl (Rev. 21:12).

Clearly, the symbolisms here find no neat correspondence. But that, precisely, is part of what intrigues me. The parallels are enough to whet the appetite and leave one breathless with excitement over their possible theological implications.

Time and again I have attempted to probe the mystery of these breathtaking conceptual and theological connections, but again and again I have found it exceedingly too subtle and complex to truly fathom, let alone put into words. It's almost as though it were meant to be apprehended "not simply by the mind but by the imagination, the heart . . ." [14]

So I am content to apprehend it as through a glass darkly. For what little I have perceived already fills my heart with sublime wonder. I stand, heart pounding and with open mouth, as if in the hallowed presence of the heavenly Shekinah and hear faintly from "within the veil" the muffled sounds of heavenly music soon to break forth as the drama of the ages comes to its exciting climax. Then we shall know, even as clearly as we are known.

---

[1] The word "extrapolation" does imply a certain degree of conjecture, but it is several notches removed from speculation because it strongly mandates that conclusions flow logically and naturally from known data.

[2] For a careful and inspiring interpretation of key aspects of the earthly sanctuary service, see *Patriarchs and Prophets*, chapter 30. I am heavily indebted to this source for this section.

[3] *Ibid.*, p. 352.

[4] *Ibid.*, p. 353.

[5] *Ibid.*, p. 354.

[6] *Ibid.*

[7] *Interpreter's Dictionary of the Bible*, vol. R-Z, p. 502.

[8] G.R.H. Wright, "Pre-Israelite Temples in the Land of Canaan," *Palestine Exploration Quarterly* 103 (1971):18.

[9] *Patriarchs and Prophets*, p. 351.

[10] *Ibid.*

[11] *Ibid.* Note the interesting case of Saul in 1 Samuel 28:6.

[12] R.C.H. Lenski, *The Interpretation of St. John's Revelation* (Minneapolis: Augsburg Pub. House, 1943, 1961), p. 640.

[13] *Patriarchs and Prophets*, p. 351.

[14] Avery Dulles, *Models of the Church* (Garden City, N.Y.: Doubleday & Co., Inc., 1974), p. 18.

CHAPTER 3

According to the Pattern

"According to all that I show you concerning the pattern of the tabernacle, and of all its furniture, so you shall make it" (Ex. 25:9, RSV).

"They serve a copy and shadow of the heavenly sanctuary; for . . . [Moses] was instructed by God, saying, 'See that you make everything according to the pattern which was shown you on the mountain' " (Heb. 8:5, RSV).

How shall we understand these scriptures? This is the issue on which we focus in this chapter.

Many Adventists insist that these passages indicate a one-on-one correspondence between the earthly sanctuary and the heavenly. In other words, a small table of shewbread in the earthly sanctuary points to a huge or grander one in the heavenly; a small incense altar here, a large one there; and so on—bread for bread, incense for incense, blood for blood, lampstand for lampstand, (metallic) cherubim for (metallic) cherubim, ark for ark.

What shall we say of such literalism? Some may feel that this understanding of the heavenly sanctuary is completely harmless. But doesn't it constitute a serious impediment in our sanctuary apologetics—that is, in the way we present the doctrine to non-Adventists and even to skeptics? More seriously, might it actually distort the message God would have us present at this time to people of every culture and of every intellectual or philosophical persuasion? Does extreme literalism help or hinder us in our attempt to focus people's attention on what we all consider to be the essence—the core—of the sanctuary message? These are important questions, I think. Surely the meaning and significance of the pattern concept invites our careful study.

At least three problems confront this extremely literalistic approach: (1) the elusiveness of the word "pattern"; (2) the existence of older (Canaanite) parallels to the earthly tabernacle/ Temple; and (3) the occurrence of dissimilarities between the wilderness tabernacle and the Israelite Temples that succeeded it.

THE ELUSIVENESS OF THE WORD "PATTERN"

In Exodus 25:9 God commands Moses to build a sanctuary according to the "pattern" (Hebrew *tabnith*)[1] of what he had seen on Mount Sinai. At first glance this seems a rather straightforward statement, hardly needing any interpretation whatsoever. God showed Moses a model of the heavenly sanctuary, then commanded him to build one like it. However, the situation is not quite that simple.

In a 1981 dissertation on the nature of biblical typology Richard M. Davidson probed the meaning of *tabnith* ("pattern") in Exodus 25:9, 40.[2] Although his burden was "to determine whether or not the original" meaning of *tabnith* implies "a vertical [that is to say, earth-heaven] correspondence," he has, nevertheless, put his finger on several other important factors relevant to the present study. Among the observations I found noteworthy for our purpose here was the wide range of interpretations to which the seemingly straightforward statements of Exodus 25:9, 40 are susceptible.

Davidson highlighted six possible interpretations of *tabnith*[3] (here contracted to five), each with its own defenders: 1. God may have shown Moses a *miniature model* of the *earthly* sanctuary, either in the form of a scale representation or in the form of an architect's plan. (In either case, Moses would not necessarily have seen the heavenly sanctuary itself.) 2. God may have shown him a *miniature model* of the *heavenly* sanctuary. (This again implies that he would not necessarily have seen the heavenly sanctuary as it really exists.) 3. Moses may have been shown *the heavenly sanctuary itself* and then was provided with a *miniature model of it* (scale representation or architect's plans) for constructing the earthly sanctuary. 4. Moses could have been shown *the heavenly sanctuary itself* and, without benefit of a miniature model of any kind, simply told to pattern the earthly sanctuary directly after it. 5. Moses was not shown either the heavenly sanctuary or any representation of it; rather, he was given a subjective vision or a burst of inspiration, the recollection of which he was to use in building the earthly sanctuary. This last view does not even require the existence of a heavenly sanctuary, though it does not necessarily deny it.

Clearly the situation is not as simple as it might have appeared at first sight. After examining the various options against the available evidence, Davidson had difficulty coming up with a clear winner. "It does not seem possible to decide with certainty . . . whether the primary reference of . . . [*tabnith*] is to the miniature model of the heavenly sanctuary, to the heavenly sanctuary itself (with a miniature model assumed), or to both." [4]

His personal view, however—with which I concur—is that Moses was given a glimpse of the heavenly sanctuary, then was "provided with a miniature model" of it "as a pattern to copy in constructing the earthly." [5] It seems to me (in agreement with Davidson) that the grandeur of the heavenly sanctuary would have been absolutely too overwhelming to be of any practical use to Moses in constructing a lowly wilderness counterpart.

If these points have been well taken, we must now grapple with the more complicated question as to the relationship, in physical and other details, between this "miniature model" (as it found actual expression in the earthly tabernacle) and the heavenly original itself. (Davidson does not address questions of this kind, since his study, as he makes clear at the beginning, is "structural [concerned with literary form and language], not . . . theological.") [6]

I suggest we proceed by briefly examining those passages in

Exodus in which the idea of building after a pattern was originally enunciated. When we do this, even in a nontechnical way, against the background of what I call "sanctified common sense," we begin to get an insight into the kind of freight that the *tabnith* idea was *not* intended to carry.

After its initial use in Exodus 25:9, *tabnith* reappears in verse 40, at the end of an extended description of the ark of the covenant, the table of shewbread, and the golden lampstands. Conceivably, someone might argue that these pieces of furniture, perhaps because of their apparent elegance, do possess sufficient dignity, so to speak, to be actually found in the heavenly sanctuary. Accordingly, this instance does not substantially help the case we are trying to build.

The third occurrence of the pattern concept comes in Exodus 26:30. Here God reminds Moses to erect the tabernacle "according to the plan [*mishpat*] for it which has been shown you on the mountain" (RSV). Although *mishpat* (meaning "judgment" or "rule"), rather than *tabnith*, is the term used in this text, the context makes it absolutely clear that we are dealing with the same idea as in Exodus 25:9, 40. *Mishpat* here is equivalent to *tabnith*.

Notice now that the pattern idea follows a detailed description of the curtains of goats' hair, boards, sockets, and bars. At this point the sensitive mind begins to wonder about the validity of assuming the presence of such mundane and purely contingent items in the heavenly sanctuary.

It is the fourth occurrence of the "pattern" idea, however, that gives our sanctified common sense its first serious jolt. Without the use this time of any special term (like *mishpat* or *tabnith*), the idea comes at the end of a description of the altar of burnt offerings. "And you shall make the altar of acacia wood, five cubits long. . . . And you shall make its horns on its four corners. . . . And you shall make its pails for removing its ashes, and its shovels and its basins and its forks and its fire pans. . . . And you shall make for it a grating of network of bronze, and on the net you shall make four bronze rings at its four corners. And you shall put it beneath, under the ledge of the altar, that the net may reach halfway up the altar. And you shall make poles for the altar. . . . You shall make it hollow with planks; *as it was shown to you in the mountain, so they shall make it"* (Ex. 27:1-8, NASB).

It seems reasonable to conclude here that though the instruments just described followed the pattern given to Moses on the mountain, such an altar, with its accessories, is not to be found in the heavens. This conclusion is confirmed by the actual outworking of the antitype. Calvary, as it must be clear to all Christians, represents the antitypical altar of burnt offerings. It is there our Lord was offered up, but how different in physical form it was from its typical counterpart!

In the type we see a sacred courtyard ringed with curtains; in the antitype, the naked, unconsecrated hill of Calvary. In the type an altar made of bronze; in the antitype, a wooden cross. In the type a sharpened knife slit the victim's throat; in the antitype, the victim's throat was untouched, but His hands and feet were pierced by Roman nails. The type reveals a hapless animal victim in the clutches of a priest; the antitype, the Son of God, Himself both the priest and victim. In the type the blood beneath the brazen altar flowed and touched its pointed horns through priestly fingers; but no one cupped that crimson stream which flowed at Calvary.

And so we may go on, if space permitted. The parallels are real, indeed, but the contrasts equally sharp and pointed. Nothing in the type portrayed the glory of that resurrection morning when Christ, the cosmic victim, rose in triumph from the grave, alive forevermore with the keys of hell and death clutched tightly in His nail-pierced hands!

The nature of the correspondence between type and antitype in this particular case is very instructive. This is the only instance in which we have been privileged to witness an antitypical fulfillment with our own eyes, so to speak, and it should serve as a corrective to our penchant for one-on-one correspondence between the earthly and the heavenly sanctuaries and their ministries. It raises the question as to whether the idea of pattern should not be understood primarily on a deeper functional and theological level.

In this connection it is enlightening to notice how the book of Hebrews handles the idea of pattern and what terms it introduces to express the concept.

In Hebrews 8:5, the author explains that the Levitical priests served "a copy [*hypodeigma*] and shadow [*skia*]" of heavenly things—an obvious reference, it would seem, to Exodus 25:40, in which God enjoined Moses to construct the tabernacle and all its appurtenances "according to the pattern [*typos* in Hebrews] which was shown you on the mountain" (Heb. 8:5, RSV).

So here three terms have been introduced: *hypodeigma*, *skia*, and *typos*. How are we to understand them?

Hypodeigma generally means "example," "model," "pattern." Here in our passage, it has the sense of "copy" or "imitation." *Skia* signifies a "shadow," or a "foreshadowing." *Typos* is correctly translated "pattern" or "model." [7]

More could be said about the meanings of these terms, but a multiplication of dictionary definitions would not materially affect the issue before us. Context is more important, for it shows how the author himself understood and used these expressions. As one studies the context, the following points become evident:

1. For the author of Hebrews, the Hebrew term *tabnith* (used in Exodus 25:40 and to which he refers as proof of his assertion) is adequately rendered by the Greek word *typos* ("pattern," "model"), else he would obviously not have employed it in translation (see Heb. 8:5).

2. *Typos*, in turn, is properly captured in the words *hypodeigma* and *skia*, for the author uses these two terms to explain the relationship between the earthly and heavenly ministries, just as he does with *typos* in the same verse (Heb. 8:5). Furthermore, my reading of the context leads me to conclude that *hypodeigma* and *skia* are used synonymously.

3. This means that *hypodeigma* and *skia*, both together as well as *separately*, are equivalents of *typos*. Thus we might properly substitute either word for *typos* in Hebrews 8:5 in translation of the Hebrew word *tabnith*.

If our reasoning so far is correct, then it is possible to go one step further. We will do this on the strength of a very significant contrast made in Hebrews 10:1. Here the limitation of the law (of sacrifices) is based on the fact that "it has only a shadow [*skia*] of the good things to come and not the very form [*eikon*] of [those] things" (NASB). So the author puts *skia* and *eikon* in sharp contrast.

Eikon, here meaning "form" or "appearance," [8] is the word the New Testament uses to translate the Hebrew *tselem* (image), a word describing the physical and spiritual correspondence between God and man in the beginning, or between father and son.[9] It is a strong word and has even been employed to describe the relationship between Christ and the Father.[10] But however strong the word, no careful Bible student would attempt to draw a portrait of God based on His reflection in humanity—or even in the earthly Jesus. A spiritual instinct deters us from such a precarious comparison.

The point is this: If a spiritual instinct deters us from dogmatizing even where we have a strong (*eikon*) correspondence, how much stronger ought to be the deterrence when there is only a *skia* (or a *typos* or an *hypodeigma*) relationship!

No wonder the apostle refers to the earthly tabernacle service as a parable (*parabole*) of the present high-priestly ministry of Christ (Heb. 9:9). Like a parable, the typical symbolisms should not be made to "walk on all fours," especially when we remember that the book of Hebrews reasons principally by *contrast* and less by *comparison*. This means that the movement is from the new to the old as much as, or even more than, from the old to the new. To put it another way, we should struggle to show not how much things in heaven resemble those on earth but how different and inferior things on earth are when set against the heavenly reality or archetype. We must never forget that "it is the heavenly and not the earthly that is the genuine. The earthly was but a pale shadow, a temporary device pointing to the real. . . . The real will explain the shadow, and not vice versa." [11]

It calls for enlightened common sense to understand that certain things follow from the concept of pattern and that other things do not. And what makes the task of discriminating most frustrating at times is that there are no fixed hermeneutical (interpretational) rules to follow.

This should not surprise us, for a large percentage of those things in Scripture that carry the deepest meaning for us is couched in figurative, symbolic language. In fact, a large part of the continuing relevance and appeal of certain cardinal truths in Scripture (the atonement, for instance) lie precisely in the figurative language through which they have been revealed to us, language that often allows them to transcend temporal, cultural, and even conceptual barriers. Let us, then, resist the temptation, springing from a misguided desire for scientific precision, to subject every scriptural symbolism to scientific analysis.

Thus it would be inappropriate to look for a mathematical, one-on-one correspondence between the earthly type and the heavenly reality. The word "pattern" cannot carry the freight with which many try to burden it.

THE EXISTENCE OF OLDER CANAANITE PARALLELS

Some years ago one of my university classmates presented a research paper in which he documented the existence of pre-Israelite pagan temple remains in Palestine, remains bearing striking resemblances to the general floor plan of the Israelite tabernacle/Temple. I can still remember his startling conclusion. "This proves," he said, "that there is no sanctuary in heaven."

His conclusion was unwarranted, of course, and the rest of the class took him to task for it. Nonetheless, the kind of evidence he discovered does present problems in some minds in regard to the concept of a heavenly pattern.

Modern archaeological discoveries in the ancient Near East have, indeed, brought to light the remains of *pre-Israelite* Canaanite temples very similar in basic form and floor structure to the wilderness tabernacle and its successor, the Jerusalem Temple. G.R.H. Wright lists several of these: the Hazor temple, built in the Middle Bronze Age (between 2000 B.C. and 1600 B.C.); the Fosse temple at Lachish, built in the Late Bronze Age (somewhere in the neighborhood of 1550 B.C.); an early "Pre-pottery Neolithic temple" at Jericho (estimated to be earlier than 3000 B.C.).[12] The one distinguishing feature, above others, is their threefold division.[13] This characteristic, among others, led John Bright to affirm that Israel's "national shrine [referring to the Jerusalem Temple] was constructed on a Canaanite pattern."[14]

J. Quellette, commenting on the Hazor and other later temples, has shown that the similarities are not nearly as striking as first meets the eye.[15] And Wright has noted that "the division . . . into three elements is not always clearly marked." Indeed, he says, "the impression given by the surviving plans of several of the buildings is that of a contrived, untidy, makeshift arrangement of insertions and additions which has not achieved fully its true form."[16]

This, however, is not quite the issue before us. The question, rather, is that there existed, at a time prior to the disclosure of the plan of the wilderness tabernacle at Sinai, non-Israelite, pagan temples that closely approximated the later Israelite equivalent both in floor plan and, as far as we can determine from the evidence, in certain accessories as well.

Were these heathen temples also designed after the heavenly pattern? Or to put it another way, if the Israelite tabernacle/ Temple was patterned after things in the heavens, why was it not unique in every way? Why was it anticipated in pagan places of sacrifice? These questions are of particular interest to people with a literalistic conceptualization of the idea of pattern.

I will suggest a possible solution toward the end of the present chapter, but perhaps it would be appropriate first to take a quick look at some of the differences existing between the wilderness tabernacle and the Temple(s) that succeeded it — the Jerusalem Temple in particular. In my judgment, this phenomenon is indirectly related to the problem of earlier heathen parallels to the tabernacle.

DISSIMILARITIES BETWEEN THE WILDERNESS TABERNACLE AND THE JERUSALEM TEMPLE

Even the casual reader browsing through the biblical description of the Jerusalem Temple notices certain structural and decorative dissimilarities between it and the wilderness tabernacle. Among these are:

1. The Jerusalem Temple contained at least two courts, not just one, as in the wilderness tabernacle.[17] (There were a "great court" [18] to which all the people had access and an "inner court" or "court of the priests" or "upper court," [19] which was mainly for the priests and Levites.)

2. There was only one entrance to the court in the wilderness tabernacle, whereas six gates led into the precincts of the Jerusalem Temple.[20]

3. The wilderness tabernacle was a collapsible, mobile tent. Solomon's Temple, for the obvious reason that Israel was now fully settled in the land, was a palatial stone edifice[21] — which gives us, perhaps, another obvious reason for not pressing too hard on the correspondence between the earthly and heavenly sanctuaries. The one existed on *earth*; the other exists in *heaven*!

4. The wilderness tabernacle contained one lampstand on the south side and one table of shewbread on the north. By contrast, the Jerusalem Temple contained 10 lampstands and 10 tables of shewbread — and on both sides, north and south (or left and right).[22]

5. Like the wilderness tabernacle, the whole Temple interior was adorned with figures of cherubim. In addition, however, the

Temple interior displayed palm trees, flowers, lions, and oxen.[23]

6. One of the courts of the Jerusalem Temple contained a large bronze sea, or tank, standing on the backs of 12 bronze oxen that faced each of the four directions of the compass. This we do not find in the wilderness tabernacle. Also, the Temple court housed 10 movable lavers instead of just one, as in the case of the tabernacle.[24]

7. At the entrance to Solomon's Temple stood two huge stone pillars called Jachin and Boaz, crowned with lilies.[25] Solomon "made chains like a necklace and put them on the tops of the pillars with a hundred pomegranates on the chains." I have not seen any speculation on the theological significance of these pillars, but they constituted one of the most noticeable differences from the wilderness tabernacle. Old Testament scholar William Shea suggests that these pillars had cressets (metallic vessels) at the top for light—something that the wilderness tabernacle did not need, blessed as it was with miraculous divine light.[26]

To these dissimilarities may be added numerous other items of lesser significance that, when combined with the obvious difference in the appearance of the two structures—one a lowly tent, the other an ornate palatial edifice, make for something that cannot simply be brushed aside by those wishing to maintain a strictly literal interpretation of building "according to the pattern."

Yet we must not forget that the Jerusalem Temple, like the wilderness tabernacle, was built according to a heavenly pattern. "Then David gave to his son Solomon the plan of the porch of the temple, its buildings, its storehouses, its upper rooms, its inner rooms, and the room for the mercy seat; and the plan of all that he had in mind, for the courts of the house of the Lord. . . . 'All this,' said David, 'the Lord made me understand in writing by His hand upon me, all the details of this pattern [*tabnith*]'" (1 Chron. 28:11-19, NASB).

Commenting on this development, Ellen G. White says that "David gave Solomon minute directions for building the temple, with patterns of every part, and of all its instruments of service, as had been revealed to him by divine inspiration." [27]

Moreover, we are sure that Solomon's builders, though contracted from a heathen nation, followed the divine blueprint, as evidenced by God's impressive demonstration of approval at the dedication of the Temple. He filled it with the cloud of His glory, "so that the priests could not stand to minister because of the cloud, for the glory of the Lord filled the house of God" (2 Chron. 5:14, NASB).

The point, then, is this: If both the wilderness tabernacle and the Jerusalem Temple were constructed according to the heavenly pattern, how can "pattern" be understood in a strictly literal sense when in so many details the two structures exhibited such striking dissimilarities? And the situation becomes even more complex when we take into account the further variations and developments indicated in Ezekiel's ideal Temple (see Eze. 40:1-43:27).[28]

Now, it may be argued that if God gave "blueprints" to both Moses and David, regardless of differences, the details in both should be considered important. This is true. But at the very least such differences ought to steer us away from dogmatizing about the exact appearance of the heavenly sanctuary based on our knowledge of the earthly. Surely a large number of the differences in detail are purely contingent, related to time and place and circumstances—the lights of Jachin and Boaz, for example. These would have replaced the supernatural light (Ex. 40:34-38) of the wilderness tabernacle. Thus the evidence leads us to the following preliminary conclusions:

1. It is not the structural details of the tabernacle/Temple that are most important. Rather, it is the basic plan. On this point, we draw attention to certain basic ingredients that characterized all three representations of the sanctuary, regardless of other variants. Among these:

   a. All three (the tabernacle, Solomon's Temple, and Ezekiel's ideal temple) faced the same direction of the compass, namely, east.[29]

    b. Each one contained three basic divisions:
        i. the court
        ii. the holy place
        iii. the Most Holy Place
    c. The basic decoration in all three was the same: the figures of cherubim adorned the interior walls.
    d. The basic equipment and furniture in each were the same—in the courtyard: the altar of burnt offerings; in the holy place: the lampstand(s), table(s) of shewbread, and the incense altar; in the Most Holy Place: the sacred ark, overshadowed by the golden cherubim.
    e. In each one, the Most Holy Place was a perfect cube.

We should look, then, to these basic structural features when seeking to draw out some of the theological meanings of the tabernacle/Temple.

2. The physical appearance of the earthly tabernacle/Temple gives us no warrant to dogmatize on the physical appearance of the heavenly original. It would seem that the safer approach is to concentrate on the *theological signification*, rather than on the *structural specification*.

This means that we do not look for heavenly counterparts for the boards and loops and sockets and grills and basins and the numerous other paraphernalia that formed part of the earthly sanctuary complex. We do not indulge in speculation regarding the significance of the kinds of animal skins used to cover the wilderness tabernacle, no more than we pontificate on the theological meaning of the stones of Solomon's Temple.

These items simply represented the building materials available at the time.[30] We should stay clear of even the gorgeous colors of the tabernacle, tempting though these may be. All this resplendency, as in the case of the colors of the high priest's dress, was "for glory and for beauty" (Ex. 28:2, 40, NASB). It would be inappropriate, for instance, to use the fact that a scarlet thread ran through the rope of all British navy ships to make theological capital out of the predominance of red in the sanctuary colors, as I have heard some Adventist preachers and expositors do (fortunately, not recently).

As I concentrate on the theological significance of the broad physical aspects of the sanctuary, I have found it helpful to think of its three basic divisions and the ritual associated with them as pointing to the three fundamental phases or dimensions of the plan of salvation, namely, *atonement, intercession,* and *judgment.* The courtyard, with its slain sacrifice on the bronze altar, signified *atonement* and pointed, in particular, to the great transaction at the cross. The holy place, with its incense on the golden altar, signified *intercession,* commencing at Christ's ascension and continuing to the end of human probation. The Most Holy Place, the focus of the great annual Day of Atonement (Yom Kippur), typified the antitypical day of *judgment,* commencing in 1844, as we shall see in a later chapter, and ending with the final eradication of sin and evil from the universe.

And all three of these together constitute Atonement with a capital A, so to speak.[31] (See diagram.)

THE THREE FUNDAMENTAL DIMENSIONS OF SALVATION PORTRAYED IN THE SANCTUARY

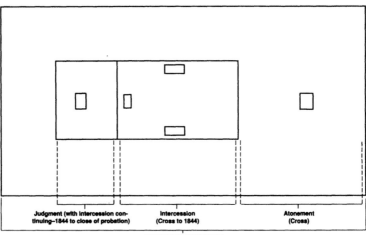

| Judgment (with intercession continuing—1844 to close of probation) | Intercession (Cross to 1844) | Atonement (Cross) |

ATONEMENT

NEED FOR BALANCE

Seen in this way, the prior existence of non-Israelite temples, similar in basic structure to the Mosaic tabernacle or the Solomonic Temple, no longer troubles us, if it ever did. The emphasis, as I have tried to show, is not primarily on the physical accessories and structure as such, but rather on the use to which they were put—their function.

It is true that we have the remains of incense stands, altars, and idols associated with these ancient non-Israelite temples, but largely unknown are the specific use to which these structures and accessories were put and, even more important, the theological meanings attributed to their services and rituals. Much of the standing furniture and other accessory paraphernalia have been lost, and the specific form of the ritual is now virtually unrecoverable. Thus we can have very little hard information as to what, in fact, transpired, the actual pattern or form of the ritual, and how the furniture and accessories related to these.

Two thousand years from now—if time lasts that long—there would not be a whole lot of difference between the remains of a Christian cathedral and a Hindu, Muslim, or Buddhist temple, especially insofar as the basic floor plan is concerned. Yet what a blunder archaeologists or theologians would commit were they then to assume from external similarity simplistic correspondence in the theology and worship of those diverse faiths!

It is entirely conceivable that God, communicating as always in human language, chose to employ a generally recognizable medium (tabernacle/Temple) for the revelation of His plan of salvation, but that in using the *form*, He drastically altered its theological meaning—its *content*.

God's concern, then, that Moses build according to the divinely revealed pattern might be seen as having a direct bearing upon this altered theological content and meaning. Accordingly, building after the pattern would not necessarily mean that Moses was to build according to the physical form of the heavenly sanctuary itself or that the structure was to be architecturally unique.[32] Rather it was more likley to show that God was careful that the major physical characteristics confirm to the blueprint provided Moses on Mount Sinai, a blueprint translated for human consumption, so to speak, and reflecting certain crucial aspects of the plan of salvation. The basic underlying idea, in other words, was that the ritual of the tabernacle, both in its daily and yearly aspects, should serve as "prophecies," symbols, types, of God's cosmic plan for human salvation and the security of the universe.

So the Israelite tabernacle/Temple, though bearing an external and superficial resemblance to things already known in the contemporary ancient Near Eastern culture, nevertheless contained important dissimilarities that pointed to momentous theological realities of things in heaven, the source and nerve center of human salvation.

---

[1] In Numbers 8:4, the Hebrew word is *mar'eh*, which means a "view" or "appearance."

[2] Richard M. Davidson, *Typology in Scripture* (Berrien Springs, Mich.: Andrews University Press, 1981), pp. 367-388.

[3] See Davidson, pp. 372-374.

[4] *Ibid.*, p. 386.

[5] *Ibid.*, pp. 378, 385.

[6] *Ibid.*, p. 10.

[7] See W. F. Arndt and F. W. Gingrich, *A Greek-English Lexicon of the New Testament and Other Early Christian Literature* (Chicago: University of Chicago Press, 1957 and 1979), s.v. *hypodeigma*, *skia*, and *typos*.

[8] *Ibid.*, s.v. *eikon*.

[9] See Gen. 1:26, 27; 5:3; cf. 1 Cor. 11:7; 15:49.

[10] Col. 1:15; cf. 2 Cor. 4:4.

[11] William G. Johnsson, *In Absolute Confidence: The Book of Hebrews Speaks to Our Day* (Nashville: Southern Pub. Assn., 1979), p. 91.

[12] G.R.H. Wright, "Pre-Israelite Temples in the Land of Canaan," *Palestine Exploration Quarterly* 103 (1971): 26, 28.

[13] J. Quellette, "Temple of Solomon," in *Interpreter's Dictionary of the Bible*, supplementary volume, p. 872.

[14] John Bright, *A History of Israel*, 2nd ed. (Philadelphia: Westminster Press, 1972), p. 222. Wright suggests that these ancient "temple types" formed "the natural background to the temple in Jerusalem" (p. 17).

[15] *Interpreter's Dictionary of the Bible*, supplementary volume, pp. 872, 873. See also Lawrence Geraty, "The Jerusalem Temple of the Hebrew Bible in Its Ancient Near Eastern Setting," in *The Sanctuary and the Atonement: Biblical, Historical, and Theological Studies*, ed. A. V. Wallenkampf and W. R. Lesher (Washington, D.C.: Review and Herald Pub. Assn., 1981), pp. 55-59.

[16] Wright, p. 25.

[17] 2 Kings 21:5; 23:12; 2 Chron. 4:9; 1 Kings 6:36; Jer. 36:10; cf. Ex. 27:9.

[18] 2 Chron. 4:9.

[19] 1 Kings 6:36; 2 Chron. 4:9; Jer. 36:10, RSV.

[20] 1 Chron. 9:18; Jer. 26:10; 36:10; 2 Kings 15:35; cf. Ex. 27:16.

[21] 1 Kings 6:7; cf. Ex. 26:1, 7.

[22] 2 Chron. 4:7, 8.

[23] I Kings 6:18, 20-22, 29-32, 35; 7:29; cf. Ex. 26:1.

[24] I Kings 7:23-39; cf. Ex. 30:18, 24.

[25] I Kings 7:21, 22; 2 Chron. 3:15-17.

[26] Personal note in my files.

[27] *Patriarchs and Prophets*, p. 751.

[28] For a description and artist's diagram of Ezekiel's Temple, see *SDA Bible Dictionary*, pp. 1074, 1075. It has been referred to as Ezekiel's "ideal temple" because, though he saw it in vision, it was never built.

[29] Ex. 17:9-16; Lev. 16:14; Num. 3:38; 2 Chron. 4:10; Eze. 8:16. The evidence that Solomon's Temple faced east is not as strong as we might wish, but it is reasonable to draw this conclusion. Second Chronicles 5:12 portrays the Levitical choir standing at the east of the (bronze) altar, a position that can make sense only if the Temple faced east. If it faced west, for instance, the choir members would have their backs either to the altar or to the sanctuary, depending on which way they were facing, both of which would have been unacceptable culturally and religiously (see Eze. 8:16).

[30] Ellen G. White explains, for instance, why the acacia wood was selected for use in the wilderness tabernacle: It was "less subject to decay than any other to be obtained at Sinai" (*Patriarchs and Prophets*, p. 347).

[31] This idea will be developed more fully in chapter 9, which deals with the atonement.

[32] The shrine (or inner shrine) would probably have represented to all ancient Near Easterners the dwelling place of God. Yahweh, in revealing the tabernacle/Temple plan to Moses/David, did not need to modify that basic concept—which probably derived originally from God anyway. We must not forget that all the peoples of the ancient Near East were related, having a common physical and spiritual stock in Noah. What we are probably seeing, then, is the distribution of a common tradition.

CHAPTER 4

Conceptualizing the Heavenly Sanctuary

How should we picture the heavenly sanctuary? The following discussion presupposes the foundation already laid in the previous chapter and seeks to probe a little deeper into the subject begun there.

Some find it easy to visualize the heavenly sanctuary as a tent pitched by the Lord, resembling the one erected by Moses in the wilderness, but of course much grander in appearance and dimension. This freestanding heavenly structure, complete with actual table of shewbread, lampstand, and incense altar, is divided, like the ancient tabernacle, into two apartments: the holy place and the Most Holy Place. A veil separates the two. The mercy seat in the inner shrine is exceedingly larger and more beautiful, of course, than its earthly counterpart and is overshadowed by (metallic) cherubim. It contains the two tables of stone and, perhaps, Aaron's rod that budded.

Let us be clear at the outset as to what we are *not* talking about. The *existence* of the heavenly sanctuary is *not* under discussion here. I think we have sufficient biblical warrant to make the categorical statement that *there is a sanctuary in heaven*, after whose ministry the earthly was patterned (see Heb. 8:1, 2; 9:1-12; cf. Rev. 11:19; 16:1). In fact, the earthly sanctuary was simply a shadow. The *real* sanctuary is in heaven, as Hebrews 8:1, 2 makes clear. In the words of William Johnsson: "While [the author of Hebrews] does not enter upon a description of the heavenly sanctuary and liturgy, his language suggests several important conclusions. First, he holds to their *reality*. . . . *Real* deity, *real* humanity, *real* priesthood—and we may add, a *real* ministry in a *real* sanctuary."[1] That question is settled so far as I am concerned.

The issue in this chapter is, rather, the kind of correspondence we should reasonably expect between the earthly sanctuary and the heavenly. It is a precarious and potentially controversial undertaking, and I must remind the reader that the ideas and conclusions put forward here represent simply my best judgment at this point. They are not to be seen as dogmatic conclusions set in concrete forever.

Anyone who has listened carefully to Adventist believers expressing themselves on the nature of the heavenly sanctuary will have observed, among other things, that the words "pattern" and "shadow" used to describe the relationship between the two sanctuaries have been understood quite literally. There is a tendency to concretize the relationship, understanding it in the sense of a literal correspondence with the heavenly original. The idea espoused is that a shadow, for example, suggests at least a form-resemblance to the physical object casting it—like the reflection of an object in the waters or the outline of an object against the light.

Accordingly, when we see a table of shewbread in the earthly sanctuary, we are to understand that that earthly "shadow" was cast by a literal, albeit grander, table of shewbread in the heavenly sanctuary. And the same for the lampstand, incense altar, ark of the covenant, and so on.

UNDERSTANDING IMAGES, FIGURES, SYMBOLS

It is generally admitted, though the full implications are not always appreciated, that God speaks to us in human language and that, more often than not, heavenly realities can be made intelligible to us only by means of images, figures, and symbols.

In one of his books on the church, Avery Dulles discusses the nature and dynamics of images in a way that could prove instructive to us at this point. "When the theologian [and, by implication, the biblical writer] uses images," says Dulles, "he does so for the purpose of gaining a better understanding of the mysteries of faith." Theologians, and biblical interpreters in general, ought to keep in mind, then, "that images are useful up to a point, and beyond that point they can become deceptive."

Thus, continues Dulles, the theologian "employs images in a reflective, discriminative way. When he hears the church called the flock of Christ, he is aware that certain things follow and others do not. It may follow, for instance, that the sheep (i.e., the faithful) hear the voice of their master (Christ), but it does not follow that the members of the church grow wool." [2] The interpreter, Dulles contends, ought always to search for "the critical principles leading to an accurate discrimination between the valid and invalid application of images." [3]

In this connection I have always been intrigued by the brevity of Jesus' interpretation of His own parables — by the way He brushes past the many *details* and *fillers* to get to the *essence*. For example, Matthew 20:1-15 presents the parable of the laborers in the vineyard using about 320 English words in the *New American Standard Bible* (some 230 words in the Greek). By contrast, the interpretation (verse 16) takes up just 10 words in the English, and nine words in the Greek. [4] We observe the same terseness in the interpretation of some biblical prophecies. [5] I would suggest that this phenomenon, though apparently unrelated, does have implications for our understanding and interpretation of the sanctuary and its rituals. We too often fail to see the forest for the trees. We have too strong a tendency to seek meaning in every board and nail.

Dulles reminds us that "when a physicist is investigating

something which lies beyond his direct experience, he ordinarily uses as a crutch some more familiar object, sufficiently similar, to provide him with reference points." He may utilize billiard balls, for instance, as models in probing the phenomenon of light.[6] Dulles then adds this significant observation: "Some models, such as those used in architecture, are scale reproductions of the reality under consideration, but others, more schematic in nature, are not intended to be replicas. They are realities having a sufficiently functional correspondence with the object under study so that they provide conceptual tools and vocabulary; they hold together facts that would otherwise seem unrelated."[7]

In line with this point of view, I would suggest that we should not conceive of the earthly sanctuary as a scale reproduction or replica of the heavenly reality. Rather the relationship ought to be seen primarily in terms of "functional correspondence," providing us with "conceptual tools and vocabulary." In other words, the earthly form puts words ("vocabulary") in our mouths, allowing us to speak about the unspeakable, to comprehend the incomprehensible, however dimly.

APPLYING THE LESSON

How, then, do we picture the heavenly sanctuary? The matter is not merely academic. It impacts the way we present the subject of the sanctuary to others and the degree of confidence we manifest as we do so.

In the previous chapter we studied the meaning and implications of the word "pattern." We singled out for special mention the one aspect of the ancient sanctuary service—the ritual in the courtyard—that found its antitypical fulfillment right here on earth, before our very eyes, so to speak. And we drew the obvious conclusion that though there was similarity in many details, there were also glaring dissimilarities.

One of the most significant of these was that the antitypical courtyard turned out to be Calvary, an unconsecrated place—not the courtyard of the earthly temple, let alone an enclosure located in heaven. In other words, this earth is the outer court of the heavenly sanctuary, a conclusion that finds support from Ellen G. White. Referring to the antitypical day of atonement, she says: "Type met antitype in the death of Christ, the Lamb slain for the sins of the world. Our great High Priest has made the only sacrifice that is of any value in our salvation. When He offered Himself on the cross, a perfect atonement was made for the sins of the people. *We are now standing in the outer court*, waiting and looking for that blessed hope, the glorious appearing of our Lord and Saviour Jesus Christ." [8]

If we draw an arrow from the ancient typical courtyard, ringed by curtains, to its antitypical fulfillment, we see the open expanse of Golgotha. If we draw an arrow from the brazen altar, with its fire pans in the ancient courtyard, to its antitypical fulfillment, we see a Roman gibbet, an uplifted cross. If we draw an arrow from the typical animal victim, burnt on the altar, to its antitypical fulfillment, we see a human figure, the Son of God, with arms extended—bleeding, dying, laid within a tomb, without broken bones or burning. Beautiful correspondences everywhere, but they are spiritual and theological—not physical and mechanical.

With this as a prime example, we can approach, conceptually, the rest of the heavenly sanctuary. We cannot know precisely what is present or what is not present there, but the kind of fulfillment that we saw in respect to the courtyard should give us a clue. Should we expect to find an altar of burnt offerings in the heavenly temple? Not at all. For a Roman cross was that antitypical altar. It was there that our Lord was slain—Himself both priest and victim.

Nor should we expect to find shewbread there from some heavenly bakery. No, the earthly shewbread "pointed to Christ, the living Bread, who is ever in the presence of God for us." [9] In other words, if we should peek into the heavenly sanctuary today, we should not expect to find a table of shewbread, but rather Him who is the Bread of Life.

We should not expect to find a lampstand, but rather Him who is the Light of the world. We should not expect to find incense burning upon an altar, but rather Him whose merits and intercession and perfect righteousness were represented thereby.[10] We should not expect to find metallic cherubim overshadowing a metallic box in an inner shrine, but rather the throne of the living God Himself, founded on justice and mercy, and surrounded by throngs of shining angels who attend Him.

Some may wonder why the book of Revelation, when referring to the heavenly sanctuary, often refers to furniture and other paraphernalia associated with the earthly sanctuary. For example, John saw the ark of the covenant in an open temple in heaven (Rev. 11:19) and, in another scene, incense bowls (Rev. 5:8). This was not to indicate, I would suggest, that this particular furniture and paraphernalia are to be found in heaven. Rather, the prophet uses these familiar objects as *codes*—or pointers—to focus our attention to the heavenly sanctuary archetype as the locus of the particular events under discussion. They say to us, in other words: "Look, we are now talking about the heavenly sanctuary."

The presence of the ark, for example, speaks of the importance and continuing relevance of the Decalogue anciently housed within it in the typical sanctuary. And it would certainly remind us also of the throne of grace, represented by the mercy seat in the ancient economy. We run into problems, however, when we insist that an actual chest—albeit a huge and glorious one—is there. Nor are we to think of an actual lamb in heaven with its throat slit and bleeding, as we might otherwise be led to assume from Revelation 5:6. Or of "souls" under an altar in heaven (Rev. 6:9).

Throughout the centuries many have stumbled over the meaning and interpretation of figurative language and symbols. Fierce theological conflicts have raged, for instance, over the meaning of the words of Jesus: "This is my body" and "This is my blood." Roman Catholics believe, even today, that these statements of Jesus speak of the real and actual body and blood of Christ, which the priest creates, so to speak, and the faithful receive during the ceremony of the Eucharist.[11]

How slow we have been to catch on! When Jesus warned His disciples to beware of the leaven of the scribes and Pharisees, He was referring to *doctrine*—not bread, as they mistakenly thought (Matt. 16:6, 11, 12). When He said, "I am the vine" (John 15), He did not mean that He was a literal plant, for He is also the Door of the sheep (John 10:7), the good Shepherd (verse 11), the Chief Cornerstone (Eph. 2:20; 1 Peter 2:6), the Sure Foundation (1 Cor. 3:11), the Rock of Ages (Matt. 16:18; 1 Cor. 10:4), the Faithful and True Witness (Rev. 1:5), the Advocate (1 John 2:1), and the Word of God (Rev. 19:13). Beautiful pictures all—to portray the matchless charms and multifaceted functions of our wonderful Redeemer!

My burden here is that we recognize the richness of biblical figures and symbols and not confuse them with the reality they portray.

NO DENIAL OF TANGIBLE REALITY

To say something is figurative or nonliteral is not to deny that there is palpable reality behind it. When I was in the Philippines, one or more typhoons would touch down there every year. Whenever one was approaching the capital, we'd hear the radio announcer say that "Public Storm Signal Number One [or Two, or Three] has been hoisted over Manila."

So far as I know, no one ever went searching for the storm signals—not even children. Perhaps in the days before radio, when communities were smaller, there might even have been a physical signal of some sort displayed in a central public area. But today everyone understands that the reference to the hoisting of a storm signal is merely a way of indicating the approach of a potentially dangerous storm and alerting listeners to its intensity.

Pity the person who, knowing the language to be figurative, thought there was nothing real or tangible to worry about and proceeded to take his family out for a sail on Manila Bay after

Public Storm Signal Number Three (the most serious of the signals) had been hoisted!

No, there is reality—tangible reality—back of the biblical figures and symbols. When the psalmist says that God will cover us with His wings, we do not understand him to be saying that God has wings like a bird. Rather we think of the protection the tiny fledgling enjoys under the wings of its mother, and we get the point (cf. Luke 13:34).

Again, recounting the dramatic rescue of Israel at the time of the Exodus, the psalmist invokes a rich array of vivid symbols— especially graphic to his contemporaries: "Thou didst divide the sea by thy might; thou didst break the heads of the dragons on the waters. Thou didst crush the heads of Leviathan, thou didst give him as food for the creatures of the wilderness" (Ps. 74:13, 14, RSV). The deliverance of Israel was real, tangible, and historical, but the images the psalmist used to describe it are figurative, nonliteral.

This phenomenon virtually permeates Scripture, for it is a universal and timeless element of human speech. In 2 Samuel 22 David recalls his days as a fugitive and describes his eventual deliverance from Saul and other enemies. His fugitive experience was real indeed, and so was his deliverance. But not so his description of them—not in every sentence. He calls the Lord, for example, "my *shield* and the *horn of my salvation, my stronghold* and my refuge" (verse 3, RSV). He recalls that "*the waves of death* encompassed me, the *torrents of perdition* assailed me; *the cords of Sheol* entangled me, the snares of death confronted me" (verses 5, 6, RSV).

Later, in the same chapter, he speaks of "the foundations of the heavens" trembling, of the heavens bowing, of God riding upon a cherub and upon the wings of the wind, with smoke streaming from his nostrils (verses 9-11, RSV).

If David felt the need to appeal to figures of speech when describing the wonder of *earthly* events and realities, should we expect less of other sacred writers as they struggled to portray *heavenly* events and scenes? Should we not give them the same poetic freedom?

When you stop to think about it, how many sentences can we make about salvation without using figurative speech? As Jesus peered through the darkness into the face of Nicodemus, He said to him: "Ye must be born again" (John 3:7). Understanding (or deliberately misunderstanding) Him literally, Nicodemus proceeded to raise scientific questions about the impossibility of a grown man reentering his mother's womb.

When Jesus offered living water to the Samaritan woman, she immediately engaged Him in a discussion of the depth of the well and His lack of a bucket to draw with (John 4:10, 11). Again and again, the Master Teacher reached for figures and similes to describe the kingdom of God: seed sowing, wheat and tares, mustard seed, leaven, hidden treasure, a costly pearl, the dragnet.

Walter Scragg in a devotional book some years ago neatly summarized what every student of the New Testament observes every day—the wide range of metaphors and similes used to describe the marvelous salvation in Jesus Christ.

"They come from differing human experiences. . . . Justification originates from the court of law. So does acquittal. Sanctification pictures the process of making a person or object holy. Redemption buys us back as a pledge is bought back. Propitiation provides one who stands in place of another.

"Jesus had His own wealth of language. He called for our conversion or turning around. In the Spirit we are born again. He puts the kingdom of heaven within us. He asks us to become as little children.

"John speaks of those who have washed their robes, of names written in the Lamb's book of life, of the victory that overcomes the world, of walking with Christ in white.

"So we might go on. The more one understands and reads, the larger the list grows." [12]

NEED FOR CALM ASSURANCE

If human speech in general and the language of salvation in particular are filled with figures and similes and metaphors, why is there the tendency to become nervous and to insist on literalism when the heavenly sanctuary comes up for discussion? Are we afraid of something? Are we concerned that some irresponsible person or group of people will destroy this fundamental belief that has become the precious heritage of Seventh-day Adventists? We need not be. No human being can destroy this doctrine. It is vouchsafed in Scripture forever.

It is with this deep, personal assurance that I approach the doctrine of the heavenly sanctuary and the language that describes it. When I see, for example, a book with the title: *The Open Gates of Heaven*, my mind at once pictures a supernal realm, portals ajar, aglow with radiant light. The mental picture is of a grander reality, engendering a ground swell of emotion and inspiration to brighten all of life.

For me, then, "the open gates of heaven" is not a statement for scientific or astronomical analysis. Rather, it is an attempt to capture the sublime in human language. It is a call to contemplation, not rationalization.

Does all this mean that there is nothing up there? that it is all an empty space? Not at all. What we need ever to keep in mind is that behind all the figures and symbols and metaphors is real, tangible reality, powerful theological truths—even behind Ezekiel's four strange creatures and wheels within wheels (Eze. 1, 2, etc.).

There are some, however, who, without saying it out loud, perceive the heavenly sanctuary as a building that God erected on some vacant lot in heaven (to put it crassly) following the entrance of sin on earth so that Jesus can minister in it. Such a conception is harmless enough, perhaps, but I doubt we would consider it worthy of serious spiritual reflection. It tends to make typical and unreal what is antitypical and real. We are not dealing with *pointers and symbols* anymore, but with the real thing.

I prefer to see the heavenly sanctuary as the dwelling place of God, the seat of His government, the nerve center of the universe. As such, it has always existed.

But with the fall of humanity it assumed an added function, namely, the solution of the cosmic rebellion and the security of the universe. It is in this sense that we picture it when we think of the ancient sacrificial system. We see it through a glass colored by the ministry for the eradication of sin.

We should realize, however, that this function is only temporary—scheduled to end when the plan of salvation is finally finished. Perhaps this is the meaning of Revelation 21:22: "And I saw no temple in the city, for its temple is the Lord God the Almighty and the Lamb" (RSV). The sanctuary, however, as the seat of God's government and His celestial dwelling place, will continue throughout eternity.

I had a seminary teacher who was a philosopher-theologian—an elderly gentleman with years of experience. He never tired of warning his students about the danger of *spiritualism*. Not simply the kind of spiritualism involving a belief in conscious survival after death, but rather the belief system that tends to dematerialize heavenly things after the manner of the ancient Greek philosophers, especially Plato, who denigrated all things physical and material. If I understand at all what I'm talking about here, *what I am proposing is as far removed from that as possible.*

That is why I do not visualize an empty heavenly sanctuary. The throne of God, in whatever form, is there, surrounded by multitudes of angels. Best of all—from our standpoint, at least—our All-sufficient High Priest, Jesus Christ Himself, is there! He fills it full! He stands before the throne of God for us! And that's enough for me!

---

[1] Johnsson, *In Absolute Confidence*, p. 91.

[2] Dulles, *Models of the Church*, p. 20.

[3] *Ibid.*

[4] The same phenomenon might be observed by comparing Matthew 21:33-42 (the parable of the landowner) with verse 43 (the interpretation); Matthew 22:1-13 (the parable of the marriage feast) with verse

14 (the interpretation); and Matthew 25:1-12 (the parable of the virgins) with verse 13 (the interpretation).

    [5] Compare, for example, Daniel 4:10-17 (about 55 lines in the *New American Standard Bible*, recounting Nebuchadnezzar's dream of the great tree) with the interpretation in verses 22, 25, 26 (about 20 lines); or Daniel 7:2-14 (about 75 lines of vision in the NASB) with verses 17, 18 (about 5 lines of interpretation). The extended additional interpretation that we find in the rest of chapter 7 came at Daniel's request (see verse 19), and, presumably, would not have been given had the prophet not requested it.

    [6] Dulles, p. 21.

    [7] *Ibid*. (Italics supplied.)

    [8] Ellen G. White, in *Signs of the Times*, June 28, 1899. (Italics supplied.)

    [9] _____ , *Patriarchs and Prophets*, p. 354.

    [10] *Ibid.*, pp. 353, 354.

    [11] See the *New Catholic Encyclopedia* (1967), s.v. "Eucharist," by W. F. Dewan. The article indicates that we "should not rely too heavily on the literalness of the words" of Jesus in Matthew 26, noting instances like John 15:1, where Jesus asserted that He is the vine. Nonetheless, in an interesting turnabout, the author maintains that it is "demonstrable that unless Christ meant the words at the Last Supper literally, the resulting metaphors would be quite confusing and worthless" (p. 602). The article deduces the literalness of Christ's words from the idea that because the Last Supper was a sacrificial meal, symbolism has to be ruled out (*ibid.*).

    [12] Walter R.L. Scragg, *Such Bright Hopes* (Hagerstown, Md.: Review and Herald Pub. Assn., 1987), p. 40.

CHAPTER 5

The Writings of Ellen G. White:

A RICH TREASURE OF IMAGES AND METAPHORS

What we have said in the preceding two chapters will not be complete—at least not for Adventists—without an assessment of what we find in Ellen G. White's writings.

In talking and listening to Adventists over the years, I have noticed a rather interesting (not to say strange) approach to the question of what is literal or what is figurative in Scripture. The Bible speaks, for instance, of the 144,000, and we all consider it proper at least to ask whether this is a literal or a symbolic number. But in the view of not a few Adventists, once Ellen G. White *repeats* the biblical figure or expression, *that* makes it literal! When we adopt this approach, we fail to notice that she herself not only repeats biblical figures and symbols without interpretation, but also uses a great many figures and imagery and metaphors of her own.

In what follows I draw attention to the richness of figures, images, metaphors, and similes found in the writings of this prolific author and messenger of the Lord. The selection is not complete by any means. It represents only a small sampling of statements that have impressed me since I began paying particular attention to this

phenomenon for purposes of this chapter. I'm sure that many
readers will come across even more significant and striking examples
during the course of their own reading.

These examples will not *prove* that my conclusions in the
preceding two chapters are correct, and I do not offer them for that
reason. Rather I present them to call attention to the figurative
richness and flexibility we find in the writings of Ellen G. White—a
flexibility that makes room for the kind of interpretation of the
heavenly sanctuary I am suggesting.

For convenience, I have divided the selection into two headings.
The first group of statements deals with general themes, the second
with the theme of the sanctuary. The emphasis in each case is my
own, inserted to call attention quickly to the figures in question. (In
almost every quotation, the reader will find other figures I did not
emphasize.)

GENERAL THEMES
1. "It is when we most fully comprehend the love of God that
we best realize the sinfulness of sin. When we see *the length of the
chain that was let down for us*, when we understand something of
the infinite sacrifice that Christ has made on our behalf, *the heart is
melted* with tenderness and contrition." [1]

How legitimate would it be to think in terms of a literal chain
let down from heaven? Or of a heart literally melting in someone's
chest upon contemplation of Christ's love? Would not Mrs. White
be utterly amazed to discover such an interpretation of her words?
Wouldn't she conclude that we had completely missed the point?
And yet this is how some people handle other figures and symbols
in her writings.

In the quotation above, the first section emphasized is clearly
equivalent to the sentence that follows it. "The length of the chain
let down for us" refers to "the infinite sacrifice that Christ has made
in our behalf." That's what Mrs. White was talking about—not
about a literal chain let down from heaven.

In most cases, however, we will not find such explanatory phrases or sentences following a particular figure or metaphor. We simply have to use our sanctified common sense to know that she does not mean that we should take her literally. This will be evident in just about all the examples that follow.

2. "By transgression man was severed from God . . . but Jesus Christ died upon the cross of Calvary, bearing in His body the sins of the whole world, *and the gulf between heaven and earth was bridged by that cross. Christ leads men to the gulf, and points to the bridge by which it is spanned*, saying 'If any man will come after me, let him deny himself, and take up his cross daily, and follow me.' " [2]

Clearly there is no physical, cross-shaped bridge between earth and heaven, no more than there is a place called "Abraham's bosom" to which the righteous go at death (Luke 16:22). Obviously Mrs. White's words were not meant to be understood literally here.

3. "Jesus became a man that He might mediate between man and God. *He clothed His divinity with humanity*, He associated with the human race, *that with His long human arm He might encircle humanity, and with His divine arm grasp the throne of Divinity*." [3]

To express the mystery of the Incarnation, she reaches into the wardrobe for her metaphor: "He clothed His divinity. . . ." Humanity is compared to a garment here.

As regards the second part of the statement, it goes without saying that the human arm of Jesus was of average length. His contemporaries saw no difference between Him and the regular Judean male. There was no evidence of giantism in Him, let alone an arm that could reach all around humanity, as though humanity were one object to be encircled in the first place. What we are observing here, then, is language rich in symbolism, and we miss the whole point if we literalize it.

4. In her book *Early Writings*, Ellen White speaks in one

place about the cruelty of the slave trade in America, making the following statement: "*Justice and judgment have slumbered long, but will soon awake.*" "*Human agony is carried from place to place and bought and sold. . . . The tears of the pious bondmen and bondwomen, of fathers, mothers, and children, brothers and sisters, are all bottled up in heaven.*"

"Said the angel, 'The names of the oppressors are *written in blood, crossed with stripes and flooded with agonizing, burning tears of suffering.*' "[4]

Here Mrs. White summons the most powerful figures of speech she could find to express her outrage over the treatment of slaves by so-called Christians in the United States. But she would be surprised if someone drew the conclusion that there are, for example, literal bottles in heaven containing the tears of battered slaves. Nor are we to imagine that the names of slaveholders are written in literal blood somewhere, or crossed with stripes, or flooded with tears. These are graphic figures of speech to express in human terms the divine outrage contained in the angel's words.

SANCTUARY THEMES

1. Referring to Christ's intercession, Ellen White says, "*He fills his mouth with arguments* in our behalf." [5]   What a graphic way of saying that Christ's every "prayer," His every wish, His every utterance, is in our behalf! But one cannot literally fill one's mouth with arguments.

2. In one of her most beautiful descriptions of Christ's intercession, Mrs. White portrays Christ as "holding before God the *censer containing His own spotless merits and the prayers, confessions, and thanksgiving of His people.*" Here again, our minds must reach beyond the literalism to the deeper truth that lies beneath. Likewise, she is in a figurative mode when she refers to the incense in the hand of Christ ascending to God as a sweet savor, "*perfumed with the fragrance of His righteousness.*" [6]

Must we think that Christ actually holds a vessel in His hand in the heavenly sanctuary? Do we imagine that His own "spotless merits" can be put into a container? Is Christ's righteousness something we can smell? How did it come about that Adventists who hold on to these literalisms are somehow regarded as more righteous, more orthodox, than those who do not? Is it not unfair to charge a fellow Adventist with not believing in a literal heavenly sanctuary simply because he or she recognizes certain similes and metaphors for what they are—beautiful portrayals of unspeakable mysteries?

3. In a dramatic example of figurative speech, Ellen G. White personifies justice and mercy and describes a cosmic meeting between them: "*Justice and Mercy stood apart, in opposition to each other, separated by a wide gulf. . . . He [Christ] planted His cross midway between heaven and earth, and made it the object of attraction which reached both ways, drawing both Justice and Mercy across the gulf. Justice moved from its exalted throne, and with all the armies of heaven approached the cross. There it saw One equal with God bearing the penalty for all injustice and sin. With perfect satisfaction Justice bowed in reverence at the cross, saying It is enough.*" [7]

The preceding example hardly needs any comments. It speaks for itself. This is figurative brilliance at its best!

Given such evident richness of literary finesse in Ellen G. White's writings, involving as it does a profuse array of figures and metaphors and similes, shouldn't we tread slowly in our attempt to attribute literalism to her? When, for example, she describes the two apartments of the heavenly sanctuary, should we come to hasty conclusions, putting her down on the side of those who espouse a strictly compartmentalized heavenly sanctuary, conforming in every particular to its earthly counterpart? Or might we not see her statements as being of the same character as those in Scripture and needing to be interpreted?

4. Ellen G. White was so free from any stale rigidity that with prophetic license, I suppose, she could link the wilderness taberna-

cle to the Christian church. In an amazing statement, she wrote: "The Jewish tabernacle was a type of the Christian church. . . . The church on earth, composed of those who are faithful and loyal to God, is the 'true tabernacle,' whereof the Redeemer is the minister. God, and not man, pitched this tabernacle on a high, elevated platform. This tabernacle is Christ's body, and from the north, south, east, and west He gathers those who shall help to compose it." [8]

So much is going on in this statement that I find it difficult to comprehend in a few words. I can only hope that readers take the time to ponder for a moment, to grasp its multifaceted richness. I would be the first to grant that Ellen White is here making a *spiritual* application—and not giving an interpretation of the sanctuary as such. But I would also suggest that her "poetic" freedom here should serve as a clue to the way she may also handle other themes that impinge on the sanctuary more directly. I think that a full understanding of what Mrs. White has done here could give us a more flexible approach to the language she uses in describing the heavenly sanctuary.

I stress again that the above statements represent only a sampling of the figurative richness found in the writings of Ellen G. White. This should not surprise us in the least. After all, all human speech is like that—even the speech of children.

One day in the Philippines I saw my 7-year-old running across the backyard. Curious, I called out to her through the window, "What are you doing, Kim?"

"Three chickens were in our yard," she said. "Three big ones! I *scared the lives out of them.*"

Only a 7-year-old, but she already understood the meaning of figurative speech. Our language would be wooden and boring without this ingredient. Everyone knows that when we say that "the car was flying down the highway" we do not mean it literally—even when, for greater emphasis, we use the word "literally," as in the statement: "the car was *literally* flying down the highway."

And even though we do this all the time—so naturally that we are not even conscious of it—no one is confused. We know instinctively when a person moves from literal to figurative and back again. When Jesus described Herod as a fox, we know that this ruler of Galilee had not turned into an animal of the dog family. Nonetheless, immediately we give face value to what follows in the same sentence: "Behold, I cast out demons and perform cures today and tomorrow" (Luke 13:32, RSV).

People everywhere, both educated and uneducated, are able to grasp Paul's meaning when he says that Israel "drank from the supernatural Rock which followed them, and the Rock was Christ" (1 Cor. 10:4, RSV). And they grasp the deeper meaning when they sing the lines:

> "Rock of Ages, cleft for me,
> Let me hide myself in Thee;
> Let the water and the blood,
> From Thy riven side which flowed,
> Be for sin the double cure,
> Cleanse me from its guilt and power." [9]

They never conclude that Christ is an actual rock with caves and crevices.

Ellen White was no different from Paul and all the others over the centuries. She used figurative language profusely and felt no need to stop to explain at every turn. No one stops for that. When she describes Jesus as pleading "My blood, Father, My blood!" [10] she does not expect us to understand that as believers around the world confess their sins Jesus continually says the same sentence to the Father day and night, night and day! No, our High Priest is not a heavenly robot endlessly repeating the same phrase like a stuck phonograph record. Instead, what she means to say is that *the very appearance of Christ the crucified one in the presence of God says*: "My blood, My blood!" There is no need for actual speech.

These things seem so obvious that they should pass without explanation, but there are literalists among us who seem to be absolutely bereft of any poetry in their blood. ("How can one have poetry in one's blood?" I can hear them say.)

Mrs. White on several occasions was obliged to respond to literalists who misinterpreted her statements about celestial things. In a passage in the book *A Word to the Little Flock*, she described scenes in the new earth and mentioned the presence of people like Abraham, Isaac, Jacob, Noah, and Daniel.[11] And in another place she spoke of visiting heaven in vision and seeing there "Brethren Fitch and Stockman . . . whom God had laid in the grave to save them." Fitch and Stockman then inquired about events on earth since their passing.[12]

"Because I speak of having seen these men," she stated in explanation, "our opponents *conjecture* that I then believed in the immortality of the soul." But "the fact of the case is that in these visions I was carried forward to the time when the resurrected saints shall be gathered into the kingdom of God."[13]

Since Mrs. White had spoken of these things as if in the past—as if they had transpired prior to her return to this dark world following her vision—some of her literalistic interpreters assumed that she was, therefore, teaching that these saints had gone straight to heaven after death.[14]

In another case, somewhat closer to the question we're dealing with in this study, Mrs. White, referring to a scene in heaven, said: "I saw two long golden rods on which hung silver wires and on the wires were glorious grapes."[15]

She was stung when people ridiculed her description as "weak and childish." She found their literalistic understanding of her words unwarranted and proceeded to offer this remarkable explanation: "I do not state that grapes were *growing* on silver wires. That which I beheld is described as it appeared to me. It is not to be supposed that grapes were attached to silver wires or golden rods, but that such was the appearance presented. Similar expressions are daily employed by every person in ordinary conversation. When we speak of golden fruit, we are not understood as declaring that the fruit is composed of that precious metal, but simply that it has the appearance of gold. The same rule applied to my words removes all excuse for misapprehension." [16]

So when Ellen G. White wants to speak of the heavenly sanctuary, she uses the references and symbolism of the earthly. She does not need, at every turn, to explain to us what she is doing. We must not base our interpretation of the heavenly reality on her mere use of language. Rather we must compare scripture context with scripture context, sprinkled with a good helping of sanctified common sense—the same sense that leads us to understand what is literal and what is figurative when we sing:

> "There is a fountain filled with blood,
> Drawn from Immanuel's veins;
> And sinners plunged beneath that flood,
> Lose all their guilty stains." [17]

Very little in that verse is literally true, but few Christians will argue about its theological power. To approach it with a wooden literalism would be to miss the point. The same is true of Mrs. White's writings.

We close this brief assessment with a statement from her pen that epitomizes all we've observed thus far. We must not explain it—for that will be to weaken it. The richness of its symbolism, the profoundness of its theology, rivals the best to be found in sacred literature. And it speaks of truths that are as real as anyone reading these lines.

"After the entrance of sin, the heavenly Husbandman transplanted the tree of life to the Paradise above; but its branches hang over the wall to the lower world. Through the redemption purchased by the blood of Christ, we may still eat of its life-giving fruit." [18]

How simple! How profound! How beautiful!

[1] Ellen G. White, *Steps to Christ* (Mountain View, Calif.: Pacific Press Pub. Assn., 1956), p. 36. (Italics supplied.)

[2] *The Seventh-day Adventist Bible Commentary*, Ellen G. White Comments (Washington, D.C.: Review and Herald Pub. Assn., 1953-1957, 1976-1980), vol. 7, p. 941. (Italics supplied.)

[3] *Ibid.*, p. 926. (Italics supplied.)

[4] _____ , *Early Writings* (Washington, D.C.: Review and Herald Pub. Assn., 1945), pp. 274-276. (Italics supplied.)

[5] *The SDA Bible Commentary*, Ellen G. White Comments, vol. 7, p. 931. (Italics supplied.)

[6] _____ , *Christ's Object Lessons* (Washington, D.C.: Review and Herald Pub. Assn., 1941), p. 156. (Italics supplied.)

[7] *The SDA Bible Commentary*, Ellen G. White Comments, vol. 7, p. 936. (Italics supplied.)

[8] *Ibid.*, p. 931.

[9] Augustus M. Toplady, in *The Seventh-day Adventist Hymnal* (Hagerstown, Md.: Review and Herald Pub. Assn., 1985), No. 300.

[10] *Early Writings*, p. 38.

[11] _____ , *Selected Messages* (Washington, D.C.: Review and Herald Pub. Assn., 1958), book 1, p. 64.

[12] *Early Writings*, p. 17.

[13] *Selected Messages*, book 1, pp. 64, 65.

[14] *Ibid.*, p. 64.

[15] *Ibid.*, p. 65.

[16] *Ibid.*, pp. 65, 66.

[17] *The SDA Hymnal*, No. 336.

[18] *The SDA Bible Commentary*, Ellen G. White Comments, vol. 7, p. 989.

CHAPTER 6

The Heavenly Sanctuary:

ITS DEFILEMENT AND CLEANSING[1]

The key text that galvanized early Adventists around the concept of the defilement and cleansing of the sanctuary was the same one that had sparked the Millerite movement from which they sprang: "And he said unto me, Unto two thousand and three hundred days; then shall the sanctuary be cleansed" (Dan. 8:14).

It occurred to these Adventist pioneers that rather than having reference to a wicked earth that needed cleansing, this cardinal scripture focused on the sanctuary in heaven. This, they concluded, was the sanctuary to be cleansed at the close of the 2300 days.

A number of questions arise in the minds of inquirers and critics as they contemplate our traditional understanding of this passage. I consider the three that follow among the most important: 1. *Are Adventists correct in making a connection between Daniel 8:14 and the cleansing of the earthly sanctuary in Leviticus 16? 2. What warrant do we have for seeing in the Danielic passage a reference to the heavenly sanctuary? 3. Why do we interject the sins of God's people into the text when the context clearly focuses on the sins of the "little horn" only?*

Because of the interconnection of these three questions, discrete answers tackling one question at a time would be well-nigh impossible without considerable repetition. However, to help the reader follow the development of the argument, I have, nevertheless, divided the chapter into these three queries, with the understanding that the response in any one segment may be incomplete and needs to be complemented by factors developed in other segments. I hope that the various pieces of this somewhat complex puzzle will all be seen to fit together toward the end.

THE CONNECTION BETWEEN DANIEL 8:14
AND LEVITICUS 16

Are Adventists correct in making a connection between Daniel 8:14 and the cleansing of the sanctuary in Leviticus 16?

My response to this question will be rather extensive, but, I hope, not too convoluted. I will proceed along four steps: (1) a brief sketch of the historical Adventist position on the defilement and cleansing of the sanctuary as found in the writings of Uriah Smith,[2] the most prolific protagonist for the sanctuary doctrine among our pioneers; (2) for the sake of contrast and perspective, an outline of the deviant position of Albion F. Ballenger;[3] (3) a brief assessment of the validity of Ballenger's position over against that of traditional Adventism; and (4) a survey of the historical-theological background of Daniel 8:14.

The point of the first three sections will be to show that *when taken together* the conflicting positions of Ballenger and the Adventist Church on the defilement and cleansing of the sanctuary reflect the biblical position more accurately than either of them separately. It will also show that, taken together, they help to clarify the relationship between Leviticus 16 and Daniel 8:14— even throwing some light on the relation of the sins of God's people to Daniel 8:14. In step 4 I will attempt to show how the book of 2 Chronicles, seen as the historical backdrop of Daniel, can serve as a conceptual bridge that helps us to see the deeper theological connection between Leviticus 16 and Daniel 8:14.

1. *The Historical Seventh-day Adventist Position*.

The historical Adventist position on the defilement and cleansing of the sanctuary is well represented in Uriah Smith. According to Smith, the cleansing of the earthly sanctuary became necessary because the sins of God's people had been transferred to it throughout the year in the course of the daily ritual.

This transference took place by means of two symbolic acts. In the first, the ancient penitent laid his hands on the head of the animal victim/representative and confessed his sins over it. In this way the defilement passed symbolically from penitent to animal victim/representative. In the second symbolic act the animal victim was killed and its blood sprinkled in a designated area of the sanctuary, thus transferring defilement from victim to sanctuary.[4] The ceremony of hand-laying would be completely meaningless, asserted Smith, apart from the concept of the transference of sin. "If nothing of this kind was intended," he argued, "the whole ministration was a farce."[5]

It was Smith's position (and that of Adventists in general) that this *symbolic* transfer of sin to the earthly sanctuary pointed to a *real* transmission of the same from the earthly penitent to the heavenly sanctuary through the blood of Jesus.[6] Adventists, moreover, have seen the concept of an antitypical or eschatological cleansing of the sanctuary in Daniel 8:14,[7] thereby affirming a close theological linkage between that text and Leviticus 16.

2. *Ballenger's Position*.

Contrary to the generally accepted Adventist view, Ballenger took the position that the sanctuary was defiled by the simple commission of sin on the part of all people and that defilement had nothing to do with confession or nonconfession. He used the following scripture, among others: "You shall also say to the sons of Israel, 'Any man from the sons of Israel or from the aliens sojourning in Israel, who gives any of his offspring to Molech, shall surely be put to death. . . . I will also set my face against that man and will cut him off from among his people, because he has given some of his offspring to Molech, *so as to defile my sanctuary* and to profane My holy name' " (Lev. 20:2, 3, NASB).

Here, according to Ballenger, the sanctuary was defiled by the sinful act itself, *before* the confession of sin. Citing Leviticus 21:9, in which the harlot daughter of the high priest profanes her father by the very fact of her harlotry (regardless of confession), Ballenger took the position that any act of sin *immediately* and *automatically* defiles the sanctuary. This is so because God, as Father of the whole human race, suffers dishonor when we sin—much as the high priest suffered shame on account of his daughter's harlotry. So considered, even the devil's sins defile the sanctuary.[8]

Ballenger went even further, maintaining that far from defiling the sanctuary, confession belongs, in fact, to the process of cleansing. A child defiles the good name of his home when he falls into crime, not when he confesses or repents.[9]

As regards the time of the cleansing of the heavenly sanctuary, Ballenger argued, this occurred at Christ's ascension, when He sprinkled His blood on the mercy seat. Thus the cleansing referred to in Daniel 8:14, which occurred centuries after the cross, has nothing to do with the sins of God's people. It refers, rather, to the sins of the devil as the instigator of sin.[10]

This, in a nutshell, was Ballenger's position on the defilement and cleansing of the sanctuary.

3. *Assessment of Ballenger's and SDA Positions.*

How should we understand the defilement and cleansing of the sanctuary—earthly or heavenly? Is the historical Adventist position correct, incorrect, or inadequate? Is Ballenger's position correct, incorrect, or inadequate?

I would like to address Ballenger's position first and (for the benefit of those who may not have read my first book on the sanctuary) begin with the conclusion I drew there. After a careful and (I hope) dispassionate examination of Ballenger's overall teaching on the doctrine of the sanctuary, I concluded that if

Adventists had adopted his position, "it could have made them the theological laughingstock of Protestantism." [11] That's how strongly I came down on Ballenger's sanctuary theology, and I have seen no reason since to modify my position.

However, the fact that Ballenger's theology as a whole was misguided and wrongheaded should not imply that it was faulty in every respect. And I have not found in Ellen G. White's condemnation of Ballenger any reference to specific items of his theology—certainly not to the particular item under discussion at this point.

So the question of assessing his position vis-à-vis the defilement and cleansing of the sanctuary remains a live one. And I would have to say, without buying in to every nuance of his position, that his basic contention as regards the defilement of the sanctuary was correct. There *is* a sense in which the sanctuary is defiled by the mere sinning of God's people (or people in general, for that matter), regardless of confession or nonconfession. There is a sense in which every sin committed defiles the heavenly sanctuary. In other words, every sin committed casts a shadow on God's government, God's wisdom, God's love—in short, on the integrity of the heavenly sanctuary, the seat of the divine administration.

At the same time, Ballenger was shortsighted in not taking into account another fundamental notion of defilement emphasized in the tabernacle ritual. When he says that confession belongs to the process of cleansing and not to that of defilement, he betrays a serious misunderstanding of the kind of defilement the Levitical service was set up to address.

The tabernacle service was designed to deal precisely with what I would call *penitential* defilement. This was the kind of defilement in which the sanctuary took responsibility for the sin of the penitent, letting him go free. It was the kind of defilement that met with God's approbation, if you please. Thus I refer to it as "penitential" or "proper" defilement. The Adventist Church, Ballenger's observations notwithstanding, has been correct in giving emphasis to this kind of defilement.

I feel thoroughly satisfied that the repeated reference to sinners appearing in the court of the tabernacle, placing their hands on the sacrificial animals, slaying them, and having their blood sprinkled on some appurtenance of the tabernacle (see Lev. 4 for many examples) had something to do with the transference of sin/defilement—the accumulation of which was cleansed or removed on the annual Day of Atonement.

And since it was God who designed and set up this ritual process and who invited Israel to bring their sins to the sanctuary, the resulting defilement was, therefore, "proper."

We should note, however, that although the sanctuary was set up to deal with penitential defilement, such defilement was clearly not "natural" to it. Hence the yearly cleansing—a cleansing that clearly pointed, in my judgment, to a great antitypical fulfillment.

The defilement that Ballenger chose to emphasize, however, is of a different category. I would call it "improper" or "rebellious" or "sacrilegious" defilement. It too is an authentic scriptural notion of defilement, and Adventists have been shortsighted in not giving sufficient attention to it. The Lord referred to it when He charged the people of Judah with setting "their detestable things in the house which is called by My name, to defile it" (Jer. 7:30; 32:34, NASB). There was no confession involved in this defilement. In the book of Ezekiel, we read about the defilement of the Temple by "foreigners" and by "the wicked of the earth" (Eze. 7:20-22, NASB). And, as we saw in Jeremiah, God charged His own people with the same crime: "You have defiled My sanctuary with all your detestable idols and with all your abominations" (Eze. 5:11; cf. Eze. 23:38; Ps. 74:7; 79:1; Zeph. 3:4).

It seems to me that any attempt to grapple with the relationship between Daniel 8:14 and Leviticus 16 must take into account *these two fundamental concepts of defilement*. Once we understand this distinction, we no longer look for easy and unwarranted connections between the two passages of Scripture. They focus on different aspects of defilement/desecration. In the Leviticus passage God gives instructions to His cooperative covenant people as to how to rid their encampment of sin's *proper* or *penitential defilement* once a year. In Daniel 8 the focus is on an entity in open rebellion against God, and what we see there is *rebellious* or *sacrilegious defilement*.

As a consequence, Daniel 8:9-13 does not fit easily into Leviticus 16, and Leviticus 16 would be out of place in Daniel 8:9-14.

Does this mean that the two passages are utterly unrelated? A wooden, rigidly scientific hermeneutic (method of interpretation) would answer this question with a yes. But a flexible hermeneutic, a hermeneutic that takes into account the implications of the dual concept of defilement explained above, would perceive an ultimate theological connection in terms of the end-time significance of the two passages, as will become clear, I hope, toward the end of this chapter.

4. *Historical-Theological Background of Daniel 8:14.*

I think another factor that has prevented many from seeing the dynamic theological connection between Daniel 8:9-14 and Leviticus 16 has been a failure to read the book of Daniel within the context of its historical-theological background.

In my judgment, one cannot fully understand the issues in the book of Daniel, particularly Daniel 8:9-14, without giving adequate attention to the historical-theological backdrop painted for us in the book of 2 Chronicles. *This book establishes a historical-conceptual bridge between Leviticus 16 and Daniel 8:9-14, which, when combined with an understanding of the dual concept of defilement, gives us an insight into the ultimate, eschatological linkage of the two passages.*

Second Chronicles was probably written by a priest—most likely Ezra—whose theological purpose in writing was to demonstrate that Judah's calamity over a period of more than 300 years of history[12] resulted from its own rebellion and insubordination, *particularly* its desecration[13] of the sanctuary or Temple, the symbol of God's holy presence in its midst. Commencing with chapter 12, the author of the book documents a recurring pattern of *desecration/judgment/restoration*, until God's patience is exhausted and He is obliged to abandon His people and sanctuary.

We may observe this phenomenon in the following chart.[14]

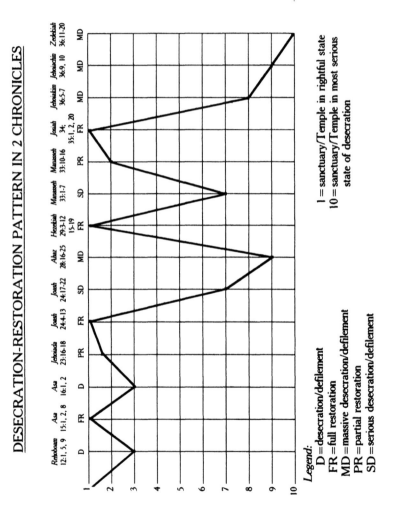

DESECRATION-RESTORATION PATTERN IN 2 CHRONICLES

1 = sanctuary/Temple in rightful state
10 = sanctuary/Temple in most serious state of desecration

Legend:
D = desecration/defilement
FR = full restoration
MD = massive desecration/defilement
PR = partial restoration
SD = serious desecration/defilement

The first defilement occurred just after the middle of the tenth century B.C. under the agency of Shishak, king of Egypt. Rehoboam (931-913 B.C.), Judah's first king after the schism,[15] was on the throne, and the sacred writer makes it clear that Shishak's desecration of the Temple resulted from Judah's rebellion against God. "It took place when the kingdom of Rehoboam was established and strong that he and all Israel with him forsook the law of the Lord. And it came about in King Rehoboam's fifth year, because they had been unfaithful to the Lord, that Shishak king of Egypt came up against Jerusalem" (2 Chron. 12:1-5, NASB).

Although the writer does not specifically refer to Shishak's action as a defilement or desecration, it obviously was, for "Shishak . . . took the treasures of the house of the Lord" (verse 9, NASB).

From this point, and through nearly 350 years, the fortunes of the sanctuary ebbed and flowed with the rise and fall of miscreants or godly rulers.

Following the desecration by Shishak, King Asa restored (Hebrew *chadash*) the Temple (2 Chron. 15:1, 2, 8, NASB).[16] However, during a period of crisis he managed to desecrate the building in a fit of panic (2 Chron. 16:1, 2).

A partial restoration under Jehoiada, the priest, followed (2 Chron. 23:16-18), then came what appears to be a full restoration, under King Joash, inspired by Jehoiada (2 Chron. 24:4-9, 12, 13). *Chadash* is used once again, accompanied by another Hebrew word, *chazaq*, meaning "to strengthen," "to fortify," "to cure," "to repair."

This restoration under King Joash was short-lived, however. For as soon as Jehoiada died, the nation reverted into rebellion, and we find a serious case of desecration under the same Joash. "And they abandoned the house of the Lord, the God of their fathers, and served the Asherim and the idols; so wrath came upon Judah and Jerusalem for this their guilt. Yet he sent prophets to them to bring them back to the Lord; though they testified against them, they would not listen" (verses 18, 19, NASB).

Among the many prophets sent to Judah at this dark point in her history was Zechariah, son of Jehoiada. Not only did the leaders of Judah reject his testimony, but they also "conspired against him and at the command of the king they stoned him to death in the court of the house of the Lord" (verse 21, NASB).

It might be noted here that Jesus, in uttering His seven woes (Matt. 23), saved the last one for those leaders who had sought to frustrate His redemptive purpose by persecuting and killing His special messengers. Of these special messengers He singled out just two by name—Abel and Zechariah, both of whom, significantly, were murdered while in the line of "sanctuary" duty (Matt. 23:29-35;[17] cf. Gen. 4:3-8).

A case of massive desecration occurred under Ahaz, one of Judah's most wicked kings. This rogue came into power with a veritable penchant for rebellion. "He burned incense in the valley of Ben-hinnom, and burned his sons in fire, according to the abominations of the nations. . . . And he sacrificed and burned incense on the high places, on the hills, and under every green tree" (2 Chron. 28:1-4, NASB).

Calamity was swift in coming—invasion by Syria and the northern kingdom of Israel. Thousands of soldiers perished, and thousands more were shamefully taken captive (verses 5-8).

But the lesson was virtually lost on Ahaz. After an abortive alliance with Assyria (verses 16-21), the king, in his distress, "became yet more unfaithful to the Lord. For he sacrificed to the gods of Damascus." Moreover, "Ahaz gathered together the utensils of the house of God, . . . cut the utensils of the house of God in pieces; and he closed the doors of the house of the Lord, and made altars for himself in every corner of Jerusalem" (verse 24, NASB).

The coming of Hezekiah to the throne witnessed a most spectacular reversal of the extensive desecration under Ahaz. "In the first year of his reign, in the first month, he opened the doors of the house of the Lord and repaired [*chazaq*] them" (2 Chron. 29:3, NASB).

Hezekiah assembled the priests and Levites, reminded them of their commitment and responsibility, and laid upon them the burden of restoring the house of God and reinstituting its worship. "Consecrate yourselves," he said to them, "and consecrate [*qadesh*] the house of the Lord" (verse 5, NASB).

Like Daniel after him (see Dan. 9), Hezekiah acknowledged the sins of his compatriots: "Our fathers have been unfaithful and have done evil in the sight of the Lord our God, and have forsaken Him and turned their faces away from the dwelling place of the Lord, and have turned their backs. . . . Therefore the wrath of the Lord was against Judah and Jerusalem, and He made them an object of terror, of horror, and of hissing. . . . For behold, our fathers have fallen by the sword, and our sons and our daughters and our wives are in captivity for this" (2 Chron. 29:6-9, NASB).

And the people responded. Levites assembled and consecrated themselves, and "the priests went into the inner part of the house of the Lord to cleanse [*taher*] it, and every unclean thing which they found in the temple . . . they brought out to the court of the house of the Lord. Then the Levites received it to carry out to the Kidron valley" (verse 16, NASB).

(It is interesting that here the word used to cover the physical restoration of the Temple by the priests and Levites is *taher*, the very word used in Leviticus 16 to refer to a purely ritual or spiritual cleansing. The words *chadash* and *chazaq* were still available to the writer, and indeed, *chazaq* is used in verse 3 regarding the repair of the Temple door. But evidently, just here he preferred *taher*, and so introduces it for the first time into the text. This probably suggests that the restoration under Hezekiah was conceived to be more radical and far-reaching than those that preceded it, involving perhaps a nonphysical [ritual] cleansing or "consecration" of the Temple as well.)

The whole society was spiritually mobilized under Hezekiah's reforms, beginning with the civic officials of Jerusalem (verses 20-24) and eventually reaching out not only to the entire southern kingdom of Judah but to the northern kingdom of Israel as well (2 Chron. 29:25-30:12). Couriers with letters signed by the king hurried north, and it is most touching to read the king's appeal to all Israel. "And the couriers went throughout all Israel and Judah with the letters from the hand of the king and his princes, even according to the command of the king, saying, 'O sons of Israel, return to the Lord God of Abraham, Isaac and Israel, that He may return to those of you who escaped and are left from the hand of the kings of Assyria. And do not be like your fathers and your brothers, who were unfaithful to the Lord God of their fathers, so that He made them a horror, as you see. . . . Do not stiffen your neck like your fathers, but yield to the Lord and enter His sanctuary which He has consecrated forever, and serve the Lord your God, that His burning anger may turn from you. For if you return to the Lord, your brothers and your sons will find compassion before those who led them captive, and will return to this land. For the Lord your God is gracious and compassionate, and will not turn His face away from you if you return to Him' " (2 Chron. 30:6-9, NASB).

Though many laughed to scorn the king's messengers, some responded (verses 10-12), and a special two-week Passover festival ensued (verses 13-23). It was truly a high point in the religious history of Judah.

Hezekiah was followed, however, by Manasseh, who led out in a fairly serious desecration of the Temple. It is remarkable that the son of such a reform-minded king should reverse so quickly and radically the spiritual gains made under his father. Not only did he rebuild the high places that his father had torn down, but, the text informs us, "he also erected altars for the Baals and made Asherim, and worshiped all the host of heaven and served them" (2 Chron. 33:3, NASB). In fact, he went even further. "He built altars in the house of the Lord of which the Lord had said, 'My name shall be in Jerusalem forever.' For he built altars for all the host of heaven in the two courts of the house of the Lord" (verses 4, 5, NASB).

To shorten, I will omit comment on the partial restoration under a reformed Manasseh (verses 10-16), followed by a further restoration under good King Josiah (2 Chron. 34:24-33; 35:1, 2, 20). By now, the *defilement/restoration/defilement* pattern we have been illustrating has probably become clear.

I end this survey, then, by calling attention to the final massive desecrations under Judah's last three kings: Jehoiakim, Jehoiachin, and Zedekiah (2 Chron. 36:5-7; 36:9, 10; 36:11-20). Each of these three kings "did evil in the sight of the Lord" (verses 5, 9, 12, NASB), and in each case Babylon became the instrument of judgment.

The priestly writer, as if to bring the whole account to a head and summarize what he has been saying all along, zeroes in on Zedekiah, Judah's last king. He did "evil in the sight of the Lord," rejecting the Lord's special messenger (Jeremiah), and rebelling against Nebuchadnezzar (verses 11-13). In that spirit of general insubordination, he was joined by both secular and religious officials, "following all the abominations of the nations." Together, "they defiled [*tame*] the house of the Lord which He had sanctified in Jerusalem" (verse 14, NASB).

The compassionate response of the Lord is emphasized again. Even at this eleventh hour He sends message after message to His people. "But they continually mocked the messengers of God, despised His words and scoffed at His prophets, until the wrath of the Lord arose against His people, until there was no remedy" (verse 16, NASB).

Only then did all hell break loose. The now-frustrated Babylonians returned in aggravated rage. Thousands in Judah were slaughtered. As for the Temple, the priestly pen painted its terrible end: "And all the articles of the house of God [not "some" as before], great and small, and the treasures of the house of the Lord, . . . he brought them all to Babylon. Then they burned the house of God, and broke down the wall of Jerusalem" (verses 18, 19,

NASB). Finally, "those who had escaped from the sword" were carried away to Babylon, *and Daniel was among them* (verse 20, NASB; Dan. 1:3, 6).

The foregoing, then, is the historical-theological background of the book of Daniel. In 2 Chronicles we see the Hebrew tabernacle/ Temple presented in a new light. Surrounded in the wilderness by an ever-vigilant guard of priests and Levites and, indeed, the entire assembly of Israel, no desecrating agent or object could venture close. Israel's sacred symbol received only that for which it was designed, namely, ritual (or penitential or proper) defilement. And its ceremonial cleansing from such *penitential defilement* once a year was adequately covered by the word *taher.*

By the time of 2 Chronicles, however, things had drastically changed. Neither priestly watchdogs nor Levitical vigilantes could deter the diabolic schemes of powerful apostate kings. The sanctuary/Temple was then subjected to malicious physical and spiritual abuse, making *taher*, by itself, clearly inadequate to depict the full dimension of the corrective measures necessary to bring it back to its rightful state. Thus we find that, while retaining *taher*, the author pressed other expressions into service: *chadash, chazaq, qadesh*. As we would do today, he reached for other terms, other expressions, to better capture the nuances of a more complex situation.

With 2 Chronicles as a backdrop, then, we are psychologically and conceptually ready for what we find in the book of Daniel, namely, an escalation and intensification of the recurrent problem we have been seeing in 2 Chronicles.

At this point we need to leave the answer hanging somewhat and proceed to the next question.

THE HEAVENLY SANCTUARY IN DANIEL 8:14

What warrant do we have for seeing in the Danielic passage a reference to the heavenly sanctuary?

In Daniel 8:3-8 the prophet sees a vision of the play and

counterplay of political powers, the first two of which (Medo-Persia and Greece) are identified in the text by name (verses 20, 21).

So as not to reinvent the wheel, I will not go into a detailed explanation of these prophecies here.[18] Suffice it to say that so far as these political powers are concerned, the vision of chapter 8 does not break new ground, but rather reiterates—with added details, of course—what has already been covered in chapters 2 (verses 31-40) and 7 (verses 1-8, 15-28).

By comparison with these two parallel sections, then, we can conclude that the third kingdom of chapter 8, signified by the "little horn" (verse 9) is the same as the fourth power of Daniel 2, represented by the legs of iron (verses 33, 40), and the fourth power of chapter 7, represented by the terrible and dreadful beast (verse 7).

If we have been correct in our interpretation that that fourth power is Rome—Rome at a point following the demise of Greece as a world power[19]—then we are in a position to pinpoint the time frame of the activities of the "little horn" of Daniel 8:10.

It seems clear that the activities of chapter 8's "little horn" parallels that of its counterpart in 7:21, 25, namely, persecuting God's people. And the significant point for our chronological emphasis here is that the vision of chapter 8 observes the "little horn" *up to* the point at which it confronts the "Prince of the host" (or "Prince of princes," verse 25), an almost obvious reference to Jesus Christ, the Prince Messiah[20]—a detail that met its fulfillment in Rome's crucifixion of our Lord at the urging of apostate leaders in Jerusalem.

But the vision of chapter 8 also tracks the nefarious activities of the "little horn" *past* the time of its confrontation with the Prince Messiah (verses 11, 12; cf. Dan. 7:25). The "continual" (Hebrew, *tamid*)[21] is "removed" by this "little horn" power, and "the place of . . . [God's] sanctuary . . . thrown down" (Dan. 8:11, NASB).

Against the background of these developments one of the holy ones asks the question "For how long is the vision concerning the continual . . . , the transgression that makes desolate, and the giving over of the sanctuary and host to be trampled under foot?" (Dan. 8:13, RSV). Put simply: How long will these atrocities against the sanctuary continue? And the answer was: "For two thousand and three hundred evenings and mornings; then the sanctuary shall be restored to its rightful state" (verse 14, RSV).

Our concern at this point is to identify what sanctuary this answer has in mind, given the chronological factors to which we have already alluded.[22]

Clearly, it would have to be a sanctuary that has theological interest for God and His people *past* the time of confrontation between (pagan) Rome and "the Prince of the host"—that is, past the time of the cross and past the time when the veil of the Temple was rent in two, a symbol of the end of the theological significance of the earthly sanctuary.

If this observation is valid, then what we see in Daniel 8:13, 14 is a shift of focus (probably unbeknown to the prophet himself) from the earthly sanctuary (or *ectype*)[23] to the heavenly sanctuary (or *archetype*).[24] Therefore, the sanctuary to be "restored," "justified," "cleansed," at the end of the 2300 "evenings and mornings" of Daniel 8:14 is not an earthly one at all, but rather a celestial.

The implication, then, is that the desecration is on a level altogether transcending anything Daniel had conceived and that the remedy needed to rectify the situation was supraphysical and supernatural. It is against this background that the prophet, under inspiration, presses the word *tsadaq* into use—to describe the reestablishment of the heavenly archetype "to its rightful state" after what the angelic messenger considered the ultimate sacrilege.

Seen in this way, the need for a linguistic connection between *taher* of Leviticus 16 and *tsadaq* of Daniel 8:14, as some would demand, does not arise.[25] In Daniel we are confronted with a desecration of cosmic proportions, so to speak, that completely dwarfed everything we encountered in 2 Chronicles put together.

SEEING IT ANOTHER WAY

The obvious message of 2 Chronicles is that the state of the sanctuary/Temple, as Daniel would have remembered it while in Babylon, was brought about by *both* the rebellious apostasy of God's own people and the defiant sacrilege of hostile pagan powers.

Daniel had a clear appreciation of these historical facts and a deep longing for the restoration of the Jerusalem Temple. In the spirit of Solomon's great dedicatory prayer,[26] he approached God in fervent supplication, with his window open toward Jerusalem. How often he must have reflected with deep remorse upon the ruined Temple in the city of his upbringing!

No wonder, then, that when the "holy one" in vision mentioned the restoration (*tsadaqa*) of the sanctuary, Daniel's sanctified curiosity immediately peaked. Naturally his thoughts went immediately to the Jerusalem Temple. How he craved the unraveling of the cryptic pronouncement: Unto "two thousand and three hundred evenings and mornings; then the sanctuary shall be restored to its rightful state"! But that, precisely, was the only major section of the vision left uninterpreted by the angel as chapter 8 comes to an end.

Hence the prophet's heartrending prayer of penitence in chapter 9. Evidently he had come to the conclusion that the time of Israel's captivity was to be lengthened (see verse 19), a conclusion probably based on the angel's mention of the "2300 evenings and mornings." If this was to be so, Daniel, though severely disappointed, would not fault God, for he had no doubt regarding who was to blame for the desolation of Jerusalem and the desecration of its sacred Temple: "We have sinned, committed iniquity, acted wickedly, and rebelled, even turning aside from Thy commandments and ordinances. Moreover, we have not listened to Thy servants the prophets who spoke in Thy name to our kings, our princes, our fathers, and all the people of the land" (verses 5, 6, NASB).

As the prophet ended this moving penitential prayer, he pleaded with God to "let Thy face shine on Thy desolate sanctuary" (verse 17, NASB). Thus Daniel's burden was for the Jerusalem Temple, and the angelic statement with reference to the sanctuary in Daniel 8:14 had been the theme uppermost in his mind and the focus of his prayer. He could hardly see beyond it.

Accordingly, when God answered him, it was to assure him that the time of Judah's captivity had not been lengthened, but that rather a further probation was to be given to his people. That probation was to amount to "seventy weeks," or, as the Revised Standard Version correctly has it, "seventy weeks of years" (verse 24). Many have recognized this as "jubilee language," meaning that Israel's probation was now set at "seventy weeks of years" — 70 x 7, or 490 years (or 10 jubilees — 49 x 10). The commencement of that period was identified in the vision itself — namely, "the going forth of the word to restore and build Jerusalem" (verse 25, RSV), or 457 B.C., as Adventists have historically calculated it.[27]

Significantly, the prophet is satisfied, even though there was really no explanation, as such, of the cryptic angelic statement of Daniel 8:14. Why? Because his nightmare had been relieved. His immediate concern was for Jerusalem and its Temple. God will keep His timetable and even extend to Israel a new probation.

It was near the close of that final probation for Israel as a chosen nation that Jesus uttered those seven woes referred to earlier in this chapter, in which He singled out by name the two leaders (Abel and Zachariah) who had died in the line of "sanctuary" duty. Coming to the end of that sorrowful litany, as if reflecting painfully upon the perennial vacillations of His people over the centuries and the vicissitudes of the sanctuary at their hands, Jesus uttered one of the most anguished cries of His entire earthly ministry: "O Jerusalem, Jerusalem, who kills the prophets and stones those who are sent to her! How often I wanted to gather your children together, the way a hen gathers her chicks under her wings, and you were unwilling. Behold, your house [your Temple] is being left to you desolate!" (Matt. 23:37, 38, NASB).

Israel had squandered its final probation. Postexilic Israel had reenacted in all its stubbornness the history of the preexilic period. The end was now upon them. The veil of the Temple would soon be torn asunder by an unseen hand (Matt. 27:51), and the focus would shift to the real sanctuary, the heavenly.

Thus the sanctuary brought to view in Daniel 8:14 is not the Jerusalem Temple at all, given the time element of the text already mentioned above.[28] And the message of the passage, as the angel was at pains to emphasize, is for *us* who are living down the stream of time from Daniel's day (see Dan. 8:26), long past the end of Israel's final probation and the utter desolation of the earthly Temple.

THE SINS OF GOD'S PEOPLE IN DANIEL 8:14

Why do we interject the sins of God's people into the text when the context clearly focuses on the sins of the "little horn" only?

The Jerusalem Temple, as we have seen, was desecrated jointly by God's ancient apostate people and the surrounding pagan nations. There can be no question about that. In the same way, God's antitypical sanctuary is desecrated jointly by God's modern apostate people epitomized in the "little horn" and contemporary secular powers, as we might infer from the broad theological strokes of Revelation 13:1-7.

But there is a third element in this scheme. To read 2 Chronicles carefully is to notice the constant presence of a faithful remnant during the apostasy. This group included people like Josiah, Jehoiada, Zechariah, Hezekiah, and Jeremiah. And there were others, like Daniel, Hananiah, Mishael, and Azariah (Dan. 1:6). It is with their spiritual descendants, the new Israel, that the Lord makes a new covenant (Heb. 8:7-12; cf. Jer. 31:31-34). His love and law control their lives. Called out from all nations, they serve Him fully, bringing no rebellious or sacrilegious defilement against His heavenly temple. Naturally, they are not the focus of Daniel 8, for that passage concentrates on *sacrilegious defilement*.

It is on this point that the Seventh-day Adventist interpretation of Daniel 8:14 has been called into question. For historically we have seen in the text the antitypical cleansing of the sanctuary from the sins of God's people, whereas the fact of the matter is that clearly the emphasis in Daniel 8 is on the sins of the "little horn."

In my judgment, there is no need for panic here. Our pioneers *did* make a hermeneutical leap at this point, and that cannot be successfully disputed. *But they did come out right!* And that, too, in my judgment, cannot be successfully explained away.

The problem that has bedeviled both Adventists and their critics, it seems to me, is the failure to take into consideration the two kinds of defilement we referred to at the beginning. Daniel 8:9-14 is dealing with rebellious or sacrilegious defilement and obviously points to a cosmic, eschatological reality. It involves God's apostate people and the nations of the world in judgment, leading to condemnation and damnation. Leviticus 16 deals with proper or penitential defilement and also points to a cosmic, eschatological reality. It involves God's penitent people in judgment leading to acquittal and vindication.

So conceived, there is an obvious convergence of these two eschatological judgments — really two aspects of the same judgment. That is why Adventists were able to make a hermeneutical leap and still come out right. The importance, however, of following a more consistent hermeneutical approach is that it allows us to develop a more comprehensive picture of the full scope and dimension of this pre-Advent judgment activity, as we shall see in chapter 8.

CONCLUSION
What then does Daniel 8:14 mean?

The key factor in coming to grips with this question is to remember that God's revelation to the prophet in Daniel 8:14, while couched against this general historical background, as we have observed, nevertheless far transcended the local conditions in Judah, Babylon, Medo-Persia, and Greece.

In other words, God was saying to Daniel: "Look, you are concerned about an earthly Temple lying in ruins in Jerusalem. You are concerned, and understandably so, about a defilement—a desecration—brought about by purely human instrumentality. However, I am pulling aside the curtain, and using the local and historical to point to the cosmic and universal.

"My purpose, Daniel, is to show that the conspiracy is much deeper than you imagine. The desecrators, the conspirators, are not mere flesh and blood, but principalities, and powers, and the rulers of the darkness of this age—spiritual wickedness in high places. The defilement, the desecration, the sacrilege, has reached cosmic proportions. It will take the action not simply of Levites and priests and godly kings to rectify it, but the action of the heavenly priest—Messiah Himself. And the importance, the scope, the intensity of the crisis demands the strongest term available to express it: *tsadaq*. Unto 2300 days, then shall the heavenly sanctuary be restored, vindicated, put back to its rightful state, *cleansed* from the stigma hurled against it by the very gates of hell, symbolized by the little horn."

Daniel 8:14, then, brings into view the fundamental fact that after centuries—yea, millenniums—of shame and abuse, God's true sanctuary is finally to be restored to its rightful state, and His name, honor, government, and people *cleansed*,[29] that is to say, vindicated forever!

---

[1] It has been generally recognized that a better translation of *tsadaq*, rendered "cleansed" in the KJV of Daniel 8:14, would be "restored" or "justified" or "vindicated." But "cleansed" (hence "cleansing") is the more familiar term. I retain it here since I see no need to make an issue of this point. Conceptually and theologically, the word "cleansing"—in the sense of "clearing" (as in "clearing one's name") really conjures the same ideas as "restoring," "justifying," or "vindicating." I will use all four terms as context and the need for variety warrant.

[2] Uriah Smith (1832-1903) played a prominent role in the development of the sanctuary doctrine in the Adventist Church. For more on his place and importance in this respect, see Adams, *The Sanctuary Doctrine*, pp. 15-35.

[3] Albion Fox Ballenger (1861-1921) was an Adventist pastor-evangelist who broke with the Adventist Church around the turn of the century over the question of the sanctuary and related doctrines. See *The Sanctuary Doctrine*, pp. 95-164.

[4] See a summary of Smith's position in *The Sanctuary Doctrine*, pp. 79-84.

[5] *Looking Unto Jesus, or Christ in Type and Antitype* (Battle Creek, Mich.: Review and Herald Pub. Co., 1898), pp. 88-90. Cf. Adams, *The Sanctuary Doctrine*, p. 79, n. 2.

[6] *The Sanctuary Doctrine*, pp. 79, 80.

[7] *Ibid.*, p. 81.

[8] Albion F. Ballenger, *Cast Out for the Cross of Christ* (Riverside, Calif.: A. F. Ballenger, 1911?), pp. 58, 59; *An Examination of Forty Fatal Errors Regarding the Atonement* (Riverside, Calif.: A. F. Ballenger, 1913?), pp. 106-112. See *The Sanctuary Doctrine*, pp. 127, 128, for a summary of Ballenger's position.

[9] See *The Sanctuary Doctrine*, pp. 127, n. 2.

[10] *Ibid.*, pp. 128-130.

[11] *Ibid.*, p. 256.

[12] Approximately 970-586 B.C.

[13] The word "defilement" no longer seems broad enough to encompass the kind of blasphemy hurled against the sanctuary in 2 Chronicles. Thus the term "desecration," which, of course, includes defilement, is pressed into service as having a wider semantic range. Out of place in Leviticus 16, "desecration" more readily captures the idea of wanton and willful sacrilege that permeates the Temple theology of 2 Chronicles and also, as will become evident later, of the book of Daniel.

[14] This diagram attempts to provide a rough summary of the vicissitudes of the sanctuary/Temple as represented in the account of 2 Chronicles. Mathematical accuracy is obviously impossible in determining the degree of either desecration or restoration. The basis of my estimate is the word picture supplied by the sacred writer. I think the chart is basically faithful to the text.

[15] The reasons for the schism in the united Hebrew kingdom of Israel are given in 1 Kings 12. See also *The SDA Bible Commentary*, vol. 2, p. 75.

[16] *Chadash* might otherwise be rendered "repair" or "renovate." It is used in Psalm 51:10, where David prays for the "renewal" of a steadfast spirit within him. The word appears too in Lamentations 5:21, where the prophet asks the Lord to "restore" His people to Himself.

[17] Note that reference here is to Zechariah, son of Jehoiada (rather than Berechiah). See *The SDA Bible Commentary* (vol. 5, p. 492) for an explanation of this variation.

[18] For the standard Adventist position, see *The SDA Bible Commentary*, vol. 4, pp. 839-847; and Desmond Ford, *Daniel* (Nashville: Southern Pub. Assn., 1978), pp. 160-193.

[19] See *The SDA Bible Commentary*, vol. 4, pp. 774, 775, 832; Ford, p. 148; G. F. Hasel, "The 'Little Horn,' the Saints, and the Sanctuary in Daniel 8," in *The Sanctuary and the Atonement*, eds. Wallenkampf and Lesher, pp. 177-208 (especially pp. 182-186).

[20] Compare Daniel 9:25. See *The SDA Bible Commentary*, vol. 4, pp. 842, 853; Ford, p. 192; and Hasel, pp. 188, 189.

[21] This term, having primary reference to the continual service in the earthly sanctuary, points in this context to the continual priestly ministry of Christ in the heavenly sanctuary. See *The SDA Bible Commentary*, vol. 4, p. 843; and Hasel, pp. 189, 190.

[22] Notice that I am deliberately avoiding the time element of Daniel 8:14 itself as the basis for my conclusion here.

[23] The terms *ectype* and *archetype* are used when an earthly symbol (ectype) points to a heavenly fulfillment (archetype). In other words, they imply a vertical direction, in contrast to "type" and "antitype," which imply a horizontal fulfillment. I have so far been using "type" and "antitype" for both horizontal and vertical fulfillments, since "ectype" and "archetype" have certain unbiblical connotations in Greek philosophy.

[24] See note 22 above.

[25] The issue we are addressing here does not turn on the particular terms used for the action of rectifying the sanctuary. We must deal more and more with context and meaning. A penchant for linguistic linkage sometimes borders on verbal inspiration and sophisticated prooftexting. Moreover, quite apart from the heightened sacrilege we've been observing (calling for more inclusive terms), we need to remember that language does experience development and that different authors, especially when separated by centuries of time, do employ different expressions for the same or similar concepts.

[26] See 2 Chron. 6:20, 21, 24-27.

[27] See Jacques Doukhan in *The Sanctuary and the Atonement*, pp. 251-269.

[28] For further information on the time element of Daniel 8:14, see W. H. Shea, *Selected Studies on Prophetic Interpretation*, Daniel and Revelation Committee Series (Washington, D.C.: General Conference of SDAs, 1982), pp. 80-88.

[29] When we talk about the cleansing of the sanctuary, we are talking about a judicial or juridical cleansing. This kind of cleansing is necessary for the sanctuary's restoration to its rightful state, for its vindication. The concepts are all part and parcel of the same package, and the translation "cleansed" eminently fits into the genius of the passage. Cf. Hasel, p. 204.

CHAPTER 7

Christy and 1844 [1]

"And he said unto me, Unto two thousand and three hundred days; then shall the sanctuary be cleansed" (Dan. 8:14).

"This hope we have as an anchor of the soul, a hope both sure and steadfast and one which enters within the veil. Where Jesus has entered as a forerunner for us, having become a high priest forever according to the order of Melchizedek" (Heb. 6:19, 20, NASB).

I n the preface of this work I made the point that the fundamental rationale for the development of doctrine is that, as human beings, we are limited and shortsighted, unable to grasp at any one time all that God means to say to us. As a result of either internal or external circumstances, the church at certain crucial points of its history becomes afflicted with a kind of theological mental block that makes it unable both to conceptualize or appreciate the full dimension of a given theological situation.

In my judgment the Millerite movement of the mid-nineteenth century, climaxing in the disappointment of 1844, was such an occasion. It was a time of great expectation and heightened spiritual fervor. Jesus was coming in a matter of years, then months, then days! In a statement written many years later, Millerite follower Hiram Edson recaptured the ecstasy among the believers as the exciting countdown neared its climax.

"We confidentially expected to see Jesus Christ and all the holy angels with Him; and that His voice would call up Abraham, Isaac, and Jacob, and all the ancient worthies, and near and dear friends which had been torn from us by death, and that our trials and sufferings with our early pilgrimage would close, and we should be caught up to meet our coming Lord to be forever with Him to inhabit the bright golden mansions in the golden home city, prepared for the redeemed. Our expectations were raised high, and thus we looked for our coming Lord until the clock tolled 12:00, at midnight." [2]

On that momentous day in October 1844, it would have mattered very little to remind the ardent Millerites of Jesus' warning that no one knows the day or the hour of the Second Advent (Matt. 24:36). They had researched the prophecies, they had taken a stand, they had alerted an unbelieving world, and tens of thousands had responded. This must be the truth, indeed, and any fresh—especially contrary—theological assessment was unthinkable. In that state of excited expectancy, perhaps not even God was able to penetrate their theological mental block, given the freedom He has always allowed us. It is October 22, and Jesus is coming back *today!*

But alas, the clock tolled 12:00 midnight, and Jesus did not come. Again, Hiram Edson: "The day had then passed and our disappointment became a certainty. Our fondest hopes and expectations were blasted, and such a spirit of weeping came over us as I never experienced before. It seemed that the loss of all earthly friends could have been no comparison. We wept, and wept, till the day dawn." [3]

It was indeed a bitter disappointment, and Edson spoke of having come close to the brink of agnosticism and apostasy. [4] But the God of the shadows, the merciful One in whom he had anchored his trust, was not far away. Despite Edson's tears, the following morning God broke through as best He could. In Edson's words: "Heaven seemed open to my view, and I saw distinctly and clearly that instead of our High Priest coming out of the Most Holy of the heavenly sanctuary to come to this earth on the tenth day of the seventh month, at the end of the 2300 days, he *for the first time* entered on that day the second apartment of that sanctuary; and that He had a work to perform in the Most Holy before coming to this earth." [5]

This position was adopted by that group of Millerites who later became known as Seventh-day Adventists. Historically it has held an important place in our system of beliefs. [6]

MEANING OF "WITHIN THE VEIL"

Edson's discovery has given rise to several important questions, the most basic of which is the following: Were our pioneers correct in saying that Jesus entered the Most Holy Place of the heavenly sanctuary for the first time in 1844, when, as Hebrews 6:19, 20 seems to suggest, He entered there immediately upon His ascension?

The answer I give to this question is: No . . . and Yes.

What do I mean by saying No, the pioneers were not correct? I mean that as one studies the statement in the book of Hebrews in the light of the use of the expression "within the veil" in the Old Testament, it would seem clear that the focus is truly on the Most Holy Place of the heavenly sanctuary *if* one accepts the idea of a two-part heavenly temple.

In my earlier book on the sanctuary I presented a detailed study of Ballenger's findings on the meaning of the veil. For convenience, let me give here a brief summary of his exegesis. [7]

Ballenger built his argument on the Old Testament usage of the Hebrew word *paroketh*. He pointed out that in all of its 25 occurrences, it always referred to the curtain dividing the holy from the Most Holy Place and *never* to the outer curtain of the sanctuary. [8] Moreover, he demonstrated that the outer curtain of the sanctuary was never designated by the term *paroketh*. Rather, the outer curtain was invariably referred to as "the door of the tabernacle" or some other expression of this kind—but never "the first veil." [9]

Of the total occurrences of *paroketh*, Ballenger drew attention to five [10] that contain the identical phrase "within the veil" and pointed out that the expressions *always* applied to the Most Holy Place. On the other hand, the expressions "without the veil" and "before the veil," occurring eight times in the Pentateuch,[11] signify, *in every case*, the holy place of the tabernacle.

Ballenger's exegesis was not flawless, and that has been noted.[12] But the flaws are minor and "leave virtually untouched his major contentions."[13]

Turning to the New Testament for a study of *katapetasma* (veil), Ballenger traced this same basic understanding through the Synoptic Gospels, noting the matter-of-fact reference to "the veil of the temple"—an obvious reference to the divider between the holy place and the Most Holy Place (see Matt. 27:51; Mark 15:38; Luke 23:45). Coming then to the book of Hebrews, he simply argued that the Holy Spirit would not contradict what He had already clearly defined in the other parts of Scripture. Thus Ballenger concluded that the expression "within the veil" in Hebrews 6:19, 20 points to the Most Holy Place of the heavenly sanctuary.

We can call attention, of course, to the fact that the book of Hebrews does speak about a "second" *katapetasma* (a second veil), but this immediately presents us with at least three problems. 1. Contrary to our well-founded Adventist approach of building a theological case on the weight of scriptural evidence, we'd find ourselves clinging for support *to a single text*, ignoring all the rest. 2. We'd be at a loss to explain why the author did not specify which veil (first or second) he had in mind in Hebrews 6:20. Why the categorical use there? 3. If we come to the place that we take just one text to prove the point, then we might be forced to maintain—on the basis of Hebrew 9:4 alone—that the altar of incense was located in the *Most* Holy Place of the earthly sanctuary, contrary to what we know from a multitude of other Bible verses.

The explanation given in the commentaries for this discrepancy in Hebrews 9:4 is intriguing but must not detain us here. Suffice it to say, the phenomenon should serve as a deterrent to any attempt to build a position on the single variation presented in the expression "second veil" in Hebrews 9:3.

In my view, then, the evidence developed by Ballenger remains basically sound *on the face of it*, and the question becomes How shall we relate to this evidence and to the conclusion that Ballenger drew from it?

There are at least three options.

One, we can decide that it would be inappropriate and unwise to take up a position on the side of a renegade who has been so vociferous in criticizing the church, especially someone whose theology Ellen G. White so strongly condemned.

Two, we can decide that his exegesis is deficient, and that regardless of the meaning of the expression "within the veil" in the Old Testament and in the Gospels, in Hebrews it *does* point to "the Most Holy Place" of the heavenly sanctuary.

Three, we may decide that, notwithstanding Ellen G. White's general condemnation of Ballenger's theology (and to my knowledge Mrs. White did not specify the particular aspects of his theology that she found offensive), he was correct in this particular. If this is so, then our pioneers, for their part, were not correct in their view that "within the veil" points to the holy place of the heavenly sanctuary.

It is perhaps clear by now that I am taking the last option. My view is that *if* the author of Hebrews was thinking in terms of "celestial geography," then our pioneers were not correct in their assertion that in 1844 Christ entered the Most Holy Place of the heavenly sanctuary for the first time. The New Testament outside the book of Hebrews, moreover, provides ample evidence that upon His ascension Christ went directly to the right hand of God, which is universally admitted to be the place of chiefest honor and was represented in the ancient tabernacle by the mercy seat in the Most Holy Place.[14]

What do I mean, then, when I say Yes, the pioneers *were*

correct? I mean that the essential point that lay beneath their choice of language was sound. Let me elaborate.

Adventists have been accused of concentrating on "celestial geography" when they teach that Christ began His ministry in the holy place of the heavenly sanctuary at His ascension and then moved to the Most Holy Place in 1844. What I have always found curious about this charge is that the very ones who thus accuse us are quick to emphasize that Christ went directly into the Most Holy Place.

Now, who is interested in this so-called celestial geography? If I say that a newly elected president of the United States spends a short period of time in Blair House around inauguration time before moving into the (newly vacated) White House across the street, I should not be accused of being interested in "Washington geography" by the person who is contending that the new president goes directly to the White House. The fact is that, if anything, we are *both* interested in "Washington geography."

However, the question—to return to the passage in Hebrews—is whether *the author of Hebrews* is at all interested in "celestial geography." And the answer, according to the evidence of the book, is that *he is not*. Nowhere in Hebrews does the author speak of a Most Holy Place of the heavenly sanctuary in contradistinction to a holy place. The contrast, rather, is always between the earthly sanctuary and the heavenly. The author is concerned to demonstrate the superiority of the heavenly sanctuary and priesthood over against the earthly sanctuary and priesthood.

In this respect the emphasis of the writer is on the idea of unlimited access. That is really what Hebrews 6:19, 20 is about. In the Old Testament, as everyone knows, only those who by accident of birth happened to be members of the tribe of Levi could claim any right of access to the sanctuary itself and its appurtenances. Moreover, of this group only the descendants of Aaron could come within the first apartment of that sacred enclosure. And then, only one man in Israel, the reigning high priest, was allowed within its inner sanctum, the Most Holy Place on earth—and even so, just once a year, on the Day of Atonement!

The astonishing truth now being brought forward in the book of Hebrews is that by means of the cross Christ has broken down every barrier. Every descendant of Adam now has full, free, and unlimited access to the throne of the living God. Every single person on earth—whatever his or her race, nationality, social standing, economic status—may now approach the throne of the Infinite Person, not with fear and trembling, but boldly, with absolute confidence, through the blood of Jesus, to receive mercy and find grace to help in time of need (Heb. 4:16; 9:11, 12, 24; 10:19, 20).[15]

This is the great assurance the apostle wanted to bring to his audience in the book of Hebrews. He shows no concern at all for "celestial geography," and this being the case, there is *no essential conflict* between the affirmation of Hebrews 6:19, 20 and the assertion of our pioneers.

ON A DEEPER LEVEL

The language of our pioneers on this issue need not embarrass us. They were not formal theologians, but ordinary men and women of the nineteenth century addressing themselves to a nineteenth-century New England audience not particularly given to thinking in abstract, philosophical terms. In fact, the mid-nineteenth century was a time when conservative Christians despised philosophy and abstract thinking.[16] They were a practical people with a practical turn of mind.

Thus the word of Scripture came to them couched in the literal symbolism of the ancient typical service, a symbolism upon which their minds were already exercised. In the midst of their overwhelming disappointment, abstract philosophical concepts would have made little sense to them.

So it was that in the providence of God they were led to fall back upon the raw and vivid literalism of the ancient typical services. God chose to meet them where they were, just as He does for us today. It was perfectly reasonable from the standpoint of the Levitical services to express the truth in the way they did. Not only did it make sense to thousands of their listeners, but it also mercifully rescued them from discouragement, apostasy, and even agnosticism, preserving their faith in God and in His promises. And the essence of the truth they thus proclaimed was much deeper than the literalistic language in which they expressed it.

There is somewhat of a parallel to this in the Christian church at large in respect to the doctrine of the atonement. In the early centuries of the Christian church, some of the Church Fathers, in describing the atonement, made use of very graphic and picturesque language. Christ, they said, disguised Himself, paid a ransom to the devil, stole into his domain, and brought deliverance to His people. Augustine even went further, using the simile of a mousetrap: As the mice are enticed into the trap by the bait, so Christ is the bait by which the devil is caught.[17] Martin Luther, the great Reformer of the sixteenth century, revived such vivid, literalistic language and used it in his preaching and teaching.[18]

This way of describing the atonement came under severe criticism on the part of some historians of dogma, who characterized it as infantile, simplistic, and grotesque.[19] But Gustaf Aulen, the respected Swedish church historian and theologian, was correct when he observed that such criticisms go "no deeper than the outward dress," and make "no serious attempt [to] penetrate behind the outward form to the underlying idea." He went on to express the view, in which I concur, that "the historical study of dogma is wasting its time in pure superficiality if it does not endeavor to penetrate to that which lies below the outward dress, and look for the religious values which lie concealed underneath."[20]

In my judgment, such sentiments are relevant to our assessment of our pioneers' description of what happened in 1844. The essence of the truth they were expressing, for those who care enough to look beneath the "outward dress," was that at the end of the prophetic period of Daniel 8:14, Christ commenced a phase of ministry that was new in kind—and one that had as its goal the final vindication of God's name and honor, the vindication of God's sanctuary and people, and the eternal security of the universe.

The problem comes when we get the impression that 140 years later we today are obligated to express this particular truth in the identical language they employed. How disappointed they would be if they should rise from the dead and discover that we had made no theological progress since their time, that we had preserved even their very utterances in formaldehyde, that we are seeing no further now than they saw then—nor any clearer!

No, we stand on their brave and inspiring shoulders now, *and without altering a single plank of the basic pillars of the faith,* we do indeed perceive a clearer vision. To maintain today that after His great victory at the cross, our spotless High Priest was confined to one section of the heavenly sanctuary—assuming there was literally such a place—for 1,800 years would be theologically incongruous and intolerable.

Perhaps a better way, then, of expressing the *same* truth that came to Hiram Edson on that tear-filled morning would be as follows: At the Ascension, Christ went into the presence of God (and in saying this, we are in line with the New Testament) and there commenced a "first-apartment ministry" (in line with the ancient typical service). At the end of the 2300 days (years) in 1844 (in line with the book of Daniel), He commenced a "second-apartment ministry" (in line with the ancient typical service on the Day of Atonement)—namely, the restoration or vindication or cleansing of the heavenly sanctuary (in line with Leviticus 16 and Daniel 8:14).

This, in my thinking, is the essence of the message that God has committed to us as a people. And as the prophetic hour struck in 1844, angels were seen in vision flying in mid-space, having the everlasting gospel to preach to them who dwell on earth—to every nation and kindred and tongue and people, announcing in clarion tones this ominous and glorious new dimension of Christ's ministry in the heavenly sanctuary: "Fear God, and give glory to him; for the hour of his judgment is come" (Rev. 14:7).

It was a misunderstanding of the scope and implications of this dramatic new phase of Christ's ministry that led to the Great Disappointment in 1844. And I believe that it will be a fuller understanding and proclamation of this new dimension of that great "second-apartment ministry" in the heavenly sanctuary which will bring nations and individuals to that long delayed rendezvous with destiny.

---

[1] I am completely satisfied in regard to the integrity of this date as the terminus of the 2300 days mentioned in Daniel 8:14. I make no defense for it here. For the historical Adventist position on this question, see Adams, *The Sanctuary Doctrine*, pp. 42-45, especially p. 43, n. 1. For a recent interpretation of Daniel 8:14 see Hasel, in *The Sanctuary and the Atonement*, pp. 177-227. For the integrity of the October 22 date for Yom Kippur in 1844, see Shea, *Selected Studies on Prophetic Interpretation*, pp. 132-137.

During World War II the British broke the Nazi military code, and Winston Churchill, deep in a bunker under the streets of London, was able to receive advance warning of Nazi military intentions. Military theoreticians might argue whether the method followed in breaking the code was correct, whether correct decoding principles, if there is such a thing, had been followed. But so far as British military practitioners were concerned, the important thing was that the code had been broken. Through divine providence, the code of Daniel 8:14 and 9:24-27 has been broken and the date 1844 has been established. If anyone has a better explanation, let him or her come forward with it.

[2] Hiram Edson, manuscript fragment. Heritage Room, James White Library, Andrews University, Berrien Springs, Michigan.

[3] *Ibid.*

[4] *Ibid.*

[5] *Ibid.*, p. 7. (Italics supplied.)

[6] See Ellen G. White, *The Great Controversy*, pp. 419-422.

[7] For a fuller explanation see *The Sanctuary Doctrine*, pp. 108-112.

[8] The reader may check the validity of this assertion by examining the following scriptures: Ex. 26:31, 33, 35; 27:21; 30:6; 35:12; 36:35; 38:27; 39:34; 40:3, 21, 22, 26; Lev. 4:6, 17; 16:2, 12, 15; 21:23; 24:3; Num. 4:5; 18:7; 2 Chron. 3:14.

[9] See *The Sanctuary Doctrine*, p. 109.

[10] See Ex. 26:33; Lev. 16:2; 16:12; 16:15; Num. 18:7.

[11] Ex. 26:35; 27:20, 21; 30:6; 40:22; 40:26; Lev. 4:6; 4:17; 24:1-3. Actually, Ballenger's total was *six* occurrences. He missed Exodus 30:6 and counted the two references in Exodus 40:22, 26 as one. See Ballenger, *Cast Out*, pp. 29, 30.

[12] See *The Sanctuary Doctrine*, pp. 109, n. 2; 110, n. 3; 144, 145.

[13] *Ibid.*, p. 145.

[14] See Mark 16:19; Acts 5:31; Eph. 1:20; Col. 3:1; Heb. 8:1; Rev. 3:21.

[15] An excellent book on this theme is *In Absolute Confidence*, by William G. Johnsson. As a quick sample of the ideas developed in that work, see pp. 116-118.

[16] This attitude might be traced back to their roots in eighteenth-century Continental pietism and Methodism. These movements represented a reaction against "the disquisitions of scholastic theologians or speculations of philosophers" (Justo L. Gonzalez, *A History of Christian Thought* [Nashville: Abingdon Press, 1975], vol. 3, p. 274; cf. pp. 287-289). See also a description of the social and religious context of life in New England in the period just before the mid-nineteenth century in Sydney E. Ahlstrom, *A Religious*

History of the American People (New Haven, Conn.: Yale University Press, 1972), pp. 373, 438, 443.

[17] Gustaf Aulen, *Christus Victor: An Historical Study of the Three Main Types of the Idea of Atonement*, trans. A. G. Herbert (New York: Macmillan Publishing Co., Inc., 1969), p. 53.

[18] *Ibid.*, pp. 103, 104, 109, 110.

[19] *Ibid.*, pp. 10, 47.

[20] *Ibid.*, p. 47.

CHAPTER 8

The Pre-Advent Judgment

Adventists have historically referred to an "investigative judgment" taking place in the heavenly sanctuary. This judgment, as we conceive it, represents the second and final phase of Christ's priestly ministry for humanity. Currently in session, it involves the examination of the individual lives of God's professed people, dead and alive.

It is perhaps safe to say that no other Adventist teaching has occasioned more ridicule and contempt than that of the investigative judgment. The reaction of non-Adventist theologians has been virtually totally negative, some seeing the doctrine as a face-saving device to explain the failure of 1844. Even within the Adventist Church itself prominent leaders have from time to time expressed strong misgivings about the concept.[1]

My assessment of this negative reaction leads me to the conclusion that the common denominator running through it all is the perception that the concept of an investigative judgment flies in the face of righteousness by faith and Christian assurance. This was clearly the case with defrocked Adventist minister-evangelist Albion Fox Ballenger.[2]

Ballenger commenced his ministry in the Adventist Church in the 1880s, a decade that saw spirited discussions of righteousness by faith among Adventists. And although it is difficult to ascertain the extent to which he was influenced by this debate, particularly as it came to a head in 1888, it is beyond question that this doctrine eventually came to dominate his theology.[3]

But (and this is very significant) whereas the 1888 debate had to do with conflicting or competing emphases on law versus grace, Ballenger's concern for righteousness by faith had little, if anything, to do with an Adventist overemphasis on law. "The basis of his indictment was, rather, Adventism's understanding of the doctrine of the sanctuary." For him, this was the heart of Adventist legalism.[4]

Accordingly, when he undertook his radical reinterpretation of the Adventist sanctuary doctrine, he sought to weed out all elements of legalism. Curiously, he retained every major component of traditional Adventist sanctuary theology, with just one exception: the investigative judgment, which he completely repudiated.[5] Like other critics of this Adventist teaching, he found it utterly inimical to righteousness by faith and Christian assurance.

JUDGMENT—A CLEAR NEW TESTAMENT TEACHING

Adventists are veterans of opposition and conflict, and our critics have repeatedly been frustrated by our ability to absorb their theological scorn. Especially does the church lend a deaf ear when the criticism is fundamentally flawed, as it is in this case. For if the notion of an *investigative* judgment is inimical to righteousness by faith and Christian assurance, then why not also the notion of judgment per se?

No one can credibly deny that judgment is a fundamental New Testament teaching. From a plethora of passages on this theme, here are a few:

"But because of your stubbornness and unrepentant heart you are storing up wrath for yourself in the day of wrath and revelation of the righteous judgment of God, who will render to every man according to his deeds" (Rom. 2:5, 6, NASB). (According to verses 7 and 8, some will receive "eternal life," others "wrath and indignation.")

"For if we go on sinning willfully after receiving the knowledge of the truth, there no longer remains a sacrifice for sins, but a certain terrifying expectation of judgment, and the fury of a fire which will consume the adversaries. . . . For we know Him who said, 'Vengeance is Mine, I will repay.' And again, 'The Lord will judge His people' " (Heb. 10:26-30, NASB).

"For we must all appear before the judgment seat of Christ, that each one may be recompensed for his deeds in the body . . . whether good or bad" (2 Cor. 5:10, NASB).

"For it is time for judgment to begin with the household of God; and if it begins with us first, what will be the outcome for those who do not obey the gospel of God?" (1 Peter 4:17, NASB).

And questions deep within us cry out for judgment. Who killed American labor leader Jimmy Hoffa? Does it really matter? Was he just a tiny dot on the landscape of eternity, to be erased without fuss or notice? Was there conspiracy in the assassinations of John F. Kennedy and Martin Luther King, Jr.? How about the perpetrators of organized crime—in particular, the trade in alcohol and other harmful drugs—who make a living by frying the brains of our youth and children and slaughtering millions on the roadways of the world by impaired drivers?

And what about white collar criminals who evade the law every day? In the late 1980s and early 1990s a huge financial scandal gripped the United States. Officials of the savings and loan associations in many states were accused of reckless investment practices over a period of years—to the tune of scores of billions of dollars.

A caustic comment on the scandal at the time by then current New York governor Mario Cuomo has implications for the larger issue of judgment and justice. Said Cuomo, "If you're a kid from

South Jamaica [Queens, New York] and you get caught stealing a loaf of bread, they'll send you to Rikers Island, and you'll be sodomized the first night you're there. But if you're a businessman ripping us off for billions, they'll go out and play golf with you."[6]

And what about the countless innocent men, women, and children taken away from their families in the dead of night—some even in broad daylight—by cold-blooded assassins and never heard from again? Is anyone to be held to account when those in power mow down unarmed, defenseless civilians? And what about the crimes committed daily against infants and innocent children—sometimes by their own parents or guardians within the privacy of their homes? Is there to be no accounting? Are the wicked miscreants of the world to go free, laughing decency and morality in the face?

Elementary human justice, quite apart from Scripture, cries out for judgment. And those who would argue that judgment is somehow inimical to Christian assurance or to the divine plan of salvation utterly misunderstand this most basic dimension of the human psyche—the demand for an accounting. And this, precisely, is what the Scriptures offer.

If our need for assurance and our emphasis on righteousness by faith, as valid as these are, obscure the biblical teaching of judgment, then we have allowed them to become an obsession. Righteousness by faith and Christian assurance are indeed fundamental New Testament teachings. But so also is judgment. We gain nothing, either theologically or experientially, by attempting to negate or neutralize any one of them.

As theologians and Bible students, we do not create theology—we discover it. This implies that we stand (or perhaps, better, kneel) before the Word and *listen*. To allow any one particular biblical emphasis to so dominate our thinking as to become a litmus test of the validity of all others is to short-circuit the listening process. This was the mind-set that led Martin Luther, that towering Reformer, to repudiate the book of James.

Theological maturity seeks to hold in balance (sometimes in tension) the various fundamental biblical themes. Thus, however much we may stress righteousness by faith and however strong our emphasis on Christian assurance, we cannot repudiate the idea of judgment if we wish to remain faithful to Scripture.

PSYCHOLOGICAL BASIS OF CRITICISM

In the light of the unequivocal New Testament affirmation of judgment, why the continued vigorous criticism of the Adventist position? My observation at this point suggests two possible reasons, both essentially psychological.

The first has to do with the currentness of the investigative judgment. Adventists have always taught that this judgment is *now* in session, an announcement potentially unnerving for anyone who has ever been summoned to appear in a human court and who still remembers the shrill voice of the clerk calling all to rise as the judge enters. Veteran attorney Louis Nizer remembers that "on the morning of the trial all the physical indicia of unbearable trepidation are evident. Hands are clammy, brows . . . wet, cheeks . . . flushed or sickly pale, eyes . . . red-rimmed, voices . . . froggy, there are artificial yawns, dry lips and . . . frequent visits to the toilet." [7]

A judgment at the end of time, or after the millennium, does not have the same psychological impact. Distance tends to minimize its terror. Even less disturbing—far less—is the theological contrivance that puts this judgment at the cross—long ago and far away.

But a judgment in session *now*? That's unnerving!

The second reason is essentially tied up with the first and revolves around the word "investigative." This word, linked to the currentness of the event, conjures up the image of Christians under surveillance by a celestial cloak-and-dagger round-the-clock investigative unit. To heighten the tension even further, some Adventists even suggest that at whatever moment this heavenly assize takes up the case of any living person, it passes a final verdict and there and then closes the probation of that individual. Should this happen at a moment when there was the indulgence of the slightest sin or mischief in the life, the person is lost forever.[8] I find it instructive that this view of the investigative judgment was the one espoused by Ballenger, who, as I indicated, eventually repudiated the doctrine entirely.[9]

Adventists who are concerned about the image of the church will see the need for refinement in those areas of our theology that easily lend themselves to misunderstanding and caricature. We can ill afford to have the church portrayed as anything less than "the repository of the riches of the grace of Christ," through which the whole universe will witness the "final and full display of the love of God." [10]

TOWARD AN EFFECTIVE RESPONSE

If we have correctly captured the reasons behind the negative reaction to the doctrine before us, then we are probably in a position to suggest a possible response. Having identified "investigative" as the buzzword in this whole debate, it would seem logical to begin by asking two things about this expression: 1. How did we come by it in the first place? 2. Is it expendable?

Origin of the expression "Investigative Judgment"—For many years I held the view that James White coined the phrase "investigative judgment," first using it in a *Review* article on January 29, 1857.[11] More recently, however, another Adventist writer has attributed its first use to a certain Elon Everts in a letter to the *Review* editor, dated December 17, 1856, and published in the issue of January 1, 1857.[12] What I now find puzzling is how an expression, appearing for the first time in a letter to the editor column on January 1, could find such a matter-of-fact usage in an article by James White only four weeks later. Clearly there is considerable ambiguity here, and more study is needed to ascertain the facts.

Be that as it may, the expression did come into general use

among early Adventists. However, it was essentially a convenience term, and not all were satisfied with it. Uriah Smith implied he would switch to more appropriate language if such could be found.[13] Evidently, however, no one was able to come up with suitable alternative terminology. And since there really was no significant agitation within early Adventism regarding its theological propriety, its use became acceptable and widespread among all our pioneers, including Ellen G. White, of course.[14]

Is the phrase expendable?—We used to speak about "Harvest Ingathering," but no longer. Today we say "Ingathering," and the program continues. We used to say, "Missionary Volunteer Society," but no longer. Today we say "Adventist Youth," and the program continues. We used to talk about the "Home Missionary Society" and then the "Lay Activities Department," but no longer. Today we talk about "Church Ministries Department," and the program continues.

We used to talk about "SAWS" (Seventh-day Adventist Welfare Service), but no longer. Today we talk about "ADRA" (Adventist Development and Relief Agency). I can still remember my consternation when I first heard of the change. "Why change when you have a good thing going?" I asked. But in retrospect I completely endorse the change. "ADRA" expresses much more comprehensively what we are about. The program continues—and better than before.

What would happen if we dropped the expression "investigative"? Or does this place us on a different level from the foregoing examples?

We pause here a moment to recognize the sensitivity of this question. It sounds so much like tampering with the fundamentals. In the view of some, any modification of our theological position, any revision of terminology, however minor—whether in the interest of clarity or precision or prudence—constitutes a betrayal of faith. But this was not Ellen G. White's position. "When God's people are at ease, and satisfied with their present enlightenment, we may be sure that He will not favor them. It is His will that they should be ever moving forward, to receive the increased and ever-increasing light which is shining for them." [15]

This does not give license, of course, to every theological crackpot who has yet another half-baked theory to foist upon the church, but it does seek to steer us away from a stale and uncritical orthodoxy.

With this in mind, we venture to suggest that "investigative" (and please note that we are dealing here with *terminology*) is not absolutely indispensable to make the case in favor of the judgment in question. And if we bear in mind the casual, informal way in which the word apparently stumbled into our Adventist vocabulary, we will not accord it more reverence than it deserves. Moreover, that the pioneers were able to make the case for several years without it ought to warn us against adopting a siege mentality on this point.

Substitute terminology—If we can ever agree to replace "investigative," there are four reasons that the expression "pre-Advent" is a good substitute. [16]

1. *Acceptance within the church*. The expression "pre-Advent," already bug-tested, [17] is currently finding growing acceptance within contemporary Adventism. It is important that those who proclaim a particular truth feel comfortable with the language used in its proclamation. Else how could they possibly do it with the greatest fervor?

2. *Apologetics*. Only eternity will reveal the vast amount of time and energy expended in years of controversy and debate over the use of the expression "investigative judgment." If such conflict is necessary, we should be prepared to wage it till the end of time. But is it really? The task of Adventist apologetics, in my judgment, is to articulate our theology in language that is clear, unambiguous, and, as far as possible, inoffensive. Our aim is communication and our goal, acceptance. Our witness is not necessarily more authentic

simply because people ridicule us. We must always ensure that we do not *deserve* the ridicule.

Accordingly, the innocuousness of "pre-Advent" is a strength. A simple attributive, it attracts no emotional attention to itself. It disarms our critics, allowing them—and us—to focus quickly and without undue distraction on the primary question at hand: the judgment. Yet at the same time it makes an essential point about this special judgment by affirming that this judgment *precedes* Christ's second coming.

3. Facility of demonstration. It has not always been easy to provide a straightforward demonstration of the particular notion of an investigative judgment in Scripture. However, the concept of a pre-Advent verdict fairly permeates biblical apocalyptic.

For example, in Daniel 12:1 we are informed of an eschatological time of crisis from which only those "found written in the book" will be rescued. And in the apocalyptic account of Matthew 24, we learn that at the time of the Parousia a loud trumpet call gathers together the "elect from the four winds" (verse 31). The contexts of these two passages clearly imply a prior determination of the spiritual standing of these individuals.

In Revelation 16 the seven last plagues, like guided missiles, pursue only those who have "the mark of the beast." Obviously there has been a prior assessment in order to affix the mark legally to some and not to others.

The locus classicus in Scripture for the concept of a pre-Advent judgment is Daniel 7. In this apocalyptic passage, the prophet observes in vision the nefarious activities of the "little horn" on earth and simultaneously views a judgment scene in heaven. He switches back and forth from earth to heaven, studying these two arresting scenes, until the notorious "little horn" is destroyed and judgment given in favor of the saints (Dan. 7:22). Arthur Ferch, in a 1979 dissertation, successfully demonstrated that these two activities transpire within historical time and that therefore the judgment of Daniel 7 is pre-Advent.[18]

One must not advance the useless argument, as do some of our critics, that since God knows everything, the concept of a prior judgment is pointless and unnecessary. Such an approach, carried to its logical conclusion, would repudiate the whole biblical notion of judgment and not simply the idea of a pre-Advent judgment. It arises from a theological shallowness that cannot penetrate beyond this visible world to worlds and systems of created intelligences who, if the universe is to be secure, must be satisfied with the integrity of the divine process of election. And the great controversy is all about the fact that such intelligences are not all friendly (Eph. 6:12; Rev. 12:7-12).

4. *Adequacy of language.* The difficulty experienced by early Adventists in coming up with a replacement for "investigative" judgment was almost certainly a result, in part, of their own restricted conception of the nature and scope of the activity involved. They perceived only the *subjective* aspect of this judgment, that having to do with our personal standing before God. Their preoccupation with this single aspect served to blind them to other important components, much as the preoccupation with righteousness by faith and Christian assurance blinds some today to the biblical emphasis on judgment.

Contemporary Adventist theologians, however, standing as they do on the shoulders of these stalwart pioneers, have grown increasingly conscious of the universal scope of this judgment activity. This has led them to question whether the word "investigative" is sufficiently comprehensive to describe it.

Especially does this become evident from a consideration of Daniel 7. Clearly in this chapter the "little horn" is a major target of the judgment. This fact alone suffices to show that this judgment has a much broader frame of reference than our pioneers were able to see in their time.

The dimensions expand even further as one compares the activities described in Daniel 7 with those of Revelation 12-14. That these two apocalyptic sections of Scripture are parallel and complementary is beyond question, as the following examples show.

a. In Daniel 7:25 God's saints are persecuted "for a time, two times and half a time" (RSV). This is answered in Revelation 12:14, where the woman—God's church—goes underground because of persecution, "for a time, and times, and half a time."

b. In Daniel 7:25 the little horn speaks "words against the most High" and continues for three and a half times (or 42 months). In Revelation 13:5, the beast speaks "arrogant words and blasphemies" against God and continues "for forty-two months" (NASB).

c. In Daniel 7:25 the little horn attempts to change times and the law. In Revelation 12:17 the dragon rages against those who keep God's law.

d. In Daniel 7:22, 25-27, the persecution of God's people is followed by judgment against their persecutor and a ruling in their favor. In Revelation 14:6ff judgment is announced against the persecutors, and a ruling (verses 12, 13) is rendered in favor of the saints.

Two things emerge from these striking parallels: (a) the judgment in Daniel 7 is post-cross, coming as it does after the end of the 42 months or 1260 years mentioned in the two accounts; and (b) the scope of this judgment is universal.

A broader scope—Revelation 12 and 13 unmask the power behind the beast (the "little horn" of Daniel 7), portraying it as the dragon, the "ancient serpent, who is called the Devil and Satan, the deceiver of the whole world" (Rev. 12:7-9, RSV; cf. Rev. 13:1-3). Through his operatives this evil genius utters blasphemies against God, God's name, God's sanctuary, and the inhabitants of heaven (Rev. 13:6). In other words, God Himself stands accused! And herein lies the *objective* side of this judgment, which our pioneers did not clearly see—or at least did not discuss.

To be sure, this judgment does separate God's true saints from the multitudes who falsely claim His name, and in this sense can perhaps be called "investigative." [19] Keep in mind that in this great

assize "books" are opened. Whatever else this means, the idea of
evaluation, of scrutiny—of *investigation*, if you like—cannot be
ignored. "Not every one who says . . . , 'Lord, Lord,' will enter
the kingdom of heaven; but he who does the will of my Father who
is in heaven" (Matt. 7:21, NASB). Evaluation is an essential part
of this judgment, and it is this aspect that impressed our pioneers.
Unnerving? Yes. But that's what the afflicting of the soul at Yom
Kippur was all about (see Lev. 23:26-32).

But the scope of this judgment is much broader and cannot be
subsumed under the word "investigative." Its wider concern is with
vindication—vindication of God's sanctuary, vindication of God's
name, vindication of God's people.

The full meaning of all this is far beyond us, of course. But
certainly the focus is the heavenly sanctuary—the seat of God's law
and government, the nerve center of human salvation. Upon its
vindication hangs the security of the universe. Hence the awesome
theological significance of that cryptic statement in Daniel 8:14:
"For two thousand and three hundred evenings and mornings; then
the sanctuary shall be restored to its rightful state" (RSV).

This is a far cry from the foot-stomping, amen-rousing pablum
of much that passes for gospel theology today. But it is a message
that takes the fullest account of reality as we know it through
experience, observation, and revelation.

The judgment now in session, then, settles the question of God's
love and justice prior to the Second Advent. It confirms the validity
and legality of the plan of salvation. And it carries in its verdict the
final vindication of God's people. It is against this background that
we are to understand the jubilant cry of that heavenly messenger in
Revelation 18:20: "Rejoice over her, O heaven, and you saints
and apostles and prophets, because God has pronounced judgment
for you against her" (NASB).

As believers in Jesus, then, we view the pre-Advent judgment
from two perspectives. Seeing it, on the one hand, as the antitype
of the ancient Day of Atonement in Israel (see chapter 6), we

"afflict our souls," realizing the solemn times in which we live. But on the other hand, with our faith firmly planted in Jesus Christ, our Great High Priest within the veil, we have absolutely nothing to fear. And understanding the whole activity from the perspective of vindication—as revealed in the books of Daniel and Revelation—we not only have nothing to fear but, indeed, have the deepest cause for rejoicing and exceeding joy.

[1] Desmond Ford has listed a whole catalog of Adventist workers alleged to have had serious reservations about the doctrine. See "Daniel 8:14, the Day of Atonement and Investigative Judgment" (unpublished manuscript, 1980), pp. 47-147 passim. Ford himself says flatly that the doctrine is not in the Bible (p. 14).

[2] See Adams, *The Sanctuary Doctrine*, pp. 104-107; cf. Ford, p. 42.

[3] See *The Sanctuary Doctrine*, pp. 104-107.

[4] *Ibid.*, p. 107.

[5] *Ibid.*, p. 137.

[6] *Washington Post*, May 27, 1990, p. A1.

[7] Louis Nizer, *My Life in Court* (New York: Pyramid Publications, Inc., 1944), p. 39.

[8] This frightful interpretation, still heard in some Adventist pulpits, fortunately cannot be substantiated in official Adventist doctrinal statements.

[9] *The Sanctuary Doctrine*, pp. 135, 136.

[10] Ellen G. White, *The Acts of the Apostles* (Mountain View, Calif.: Pacific Press Pub. Assn., 1911), p. 9.

[11] *The Sanctuary Doctrine*, p. 81, n. 3.

[12] Paul Gordon, *The Sanctuary, 1844, and the Pioneers* (Washington, D.C.: Review and Herald Pub. Assn., 1983), p. 87.

[13] See Smith, "The Sanctuary," *Review and Herald*, Sept. 27, 1887. Cf. *The Sanctuary Doctrine*, p. 81, n. 3. Evidently God did not see fit to reveal a special replacement term to His prophet. Given the many issues swirling at the time, this was clearly not a matter of urgency. So Mrs. White used the term available to her. We need not conclude, however, that her use of the term makes it irreplaceable.

[14] *Ibid.*

[15] E. G. White, *Counsels to Writers and Editors*, p. 41.

[16] I already made this suggestion in *The Sanctuary Doctrine*, pp. 260-262.

[17] The word has been in use in Adventist circles for at least 30 years. See W. E. Read in *Doctrinal Discussions* (Washington, D.C.: Review and Herald Pub. Assn., n.d.) chaps. 3 and 4. This book is a compilation of special *Ministry* articles appearing in 1960 and 1961.

[18] See Arthur Ferch, *The Son of Man in Daniel 7* (Berrien Springs, Mich.: Andrews University Press, 1979). For a summary of this evidence, see Ferch, "The Pre-Advent Judgment," *Adventist Review*, Oct. 30, 1980, pp. 4-6.

[19] We probably need to recognize, however, that the idea of an "investigative judgment" is not a viable one in human jurisprudence. According to the law of most countries, an investigation (usually done by the police, the military, or a grand jury) precedes the actual judgment and is not a part of it. A judge (or court) then assesses and evaluates the evidence gathered in an investigation. However, one can make the point that this is not a human court and that therefore the investigation, being flawless, is itself the judgment. This is why I do not suggest that we abandon the expression altogether but simply that we limit its use to just one phase of the pre-Advent judgment.

CHAPTER 9

One Pulse of Harmony:

THE CONSUMMATION OF ATONEMENT

S ome have charged that the Adventist position on the atonement flies in the face of the gospel and constitutes a prostitution of righteousness by faith. As I write these lines, I recall two couples in particular — very dear friends of mine (as a matter of fact, I was privileged to conduct the wedding service for the younger of the two couples) — who have left the Adventist Church over this and related questions.

In the case of the older of the two couples, I have been particularly distressed to note that two of their very talented children have also moved away from the close fellowship that we once shared together in the local church.

I have found it difficult to reason with friends like these. What does one say to people who still keep the Sabbath and who believe they are walking more closely to Jesus now than they ever did? What *can* one say to them? Yet I know from the story of movements such as the one that now enjoys their fellowship that sorrow and disappointment probably await them down the road.

What I write in this chapter is part of what I would like to say to them and all others similarly situated. Some of the things I will say may sound theoretical, but I think they impinge on very real issues and questions that some (maybe many) of our people are facing today.

AN OPEN LETTER

Some years ago the president of the Central Luzon Mission in the Philippines (now deceased) received an open letter signed by three of his constituents. The letter called attention to two objections to "the Seventh-day Adventists [sic] 1844 theology." One of these objections had to do with the doctrine of the atonement and contended that the Adventist teaching on this subject is "incompatible with the gospel of Christ."

Elaborating further, the letter says: "This objection is based on the premise that the atonement was completed at the cross. The apostolic gospel proclaims a finished work of redemption. It is the good news of Christ's finished work. He has made atonement for sin (Rom. 3:25; 1 John 2:2), destroyed death (2 Tim. 1:10), and defeated the devil (Heb. 2:14)." [1]

Calling attention to the Adventist belief in a "final" atonement in the heavenly sanctuary since 1844, these brethren made the point that "if the atonement was completed at the cross, then any subsequent act of atonement, [whether you] call it final or special atonement, is unacceptable." Precisely this, however, was the position of the pioneers of Adventism, contends the open letter, naming in particular Uriah Smith and Ellen G. White. [2]

So in this assessment of the Adventist position on the atonement, I begin by drawing attention to the positions held by Uriah Smith and Ellen G. White, the two leaders highlighted in the open letter and who, indeed, were among the most influential of our pioneers.

URIAH SMITH'S POSITION

Uriah Smith was emphatic in expressing his position on the atonement, and the letter quoted him correctly: "Christ did not make the atonement when He shed His blood upon the cross." And in typical Uriahan style he added, "Let this fact be fixed forever in the mind."[3] This statement fairly represents Uriah Smith's position on the atonement in relation to the cross.[4]

However, as one reads more widely in Uriah Smith's writings, one develops a feel for what he was trying to say. Certainly the above sentiment, and many others in the same vein, must not be interpreted as belittling in any way the importance and centrality of the cross on Smith's part. The fact of the matter is that for him the death of Christ on the cross was all-sufficient as a sacrifice for sin. But—and this is the point to note—he did not regard that act as the atonement.

Smith based his position on a rigid interpretation of the ancient typical system. In the Old Testament sacrificial system he saw the atonement as something occurring within the sanctuary once a year. Accordingly, he believed that the locus of the antitypical atonement should likewise be within the sanctuary. In that case, of course, the heavenly sanctuary.

Now, the open letter might have been more sensitive to this motivation. It might have noted that Smith's strong denial of a finished atonement at the cross was related, in part, to terminology and definition. On the other hand, in fairness to the writers of the open letter, we would have to admit that there was really no obligation on their part to bend over backward for the sake of Uriah Smith. The letter stated his position accurately. Smith was, indeed, in error on this point.

ELLEN G. WHITE'S POSITION

In the statements from Ellen G. White, cited in the open letter, she does seem to take a position identical with that of Smith: "By His death He began that work which after His resurrection He ascended to complete in heaven."[5] And in another place she says that "before Christ's work for the redemption of men is completed there is a work of atonement for the removal of sin from the sanctuary." [6]

Clearly these statements imply a continuing atonement in the heavenly sanctuary and therefore, by implication, an incomplete atonement at the cross.

But it seems patently unfair to the total evidence to arrive at a finding that Ellen G. White was at one with Uriah Smith in regard to the atonement at the cross or that she taught an incomplete atonement at the cross.

Notice these powerful statements from her pen: "The seal of heaven has been affixed to Christ's atonement. His sacrifice is in every way satisfactory." [7] And speaking about the ascension of our Lord in the same article, she said: "The time had come for the universe of heaven to accept their King. Angels, cherubim, and seraphim would now stand in view of the cross. . . . No language could convey the rejoicing of heaven or of God's expression of satisfaction and delight in His only-begotten Son as He saw the *completion* of the atonement." [8]

And there is more. "When He offered Himself on the cross, a *perfect atonement* was made for the sins of the people." [9]

And yet again: "Christ's words on the mountainside were the announcements that His sacrifice in behalf of man was full and complete. *The conditions of the atonement had been fulfilled*; the work for which He came to this world had been accomplished." [10]

The following statement ties it all together: "He planted the cross between heaven and earth, and when the Father beheld the sacrifice of His Son, He bowed before it in recognition of its perfection. 'It is enough,' He said. 'The atonement is complete.' " [11]

These are strong affirmations of a finished atonement at the cross, and the open letter could only make its case by ignoring them. Obviously, what we have in Ellen G. White is the conception of an atonement embracing two fundamental components—one component reaching its climax at the cross and the second component transpiring and continuing in the heavenly sanctuary.

The question to ask is whether or not this understanding is correct, a question that naturally leads us into a brief summary of the biblical idea of atonement as well as the conception of the atonement in the history of Christian thought.

THE BIBLICAL IDEA OF ATONEMENT[12]

The Hebrew word for atonement is *kippurim* and derives from the verb *kaphar*. Though occurring frequently in the Old Testament, the exact connotation of *kaphar* is still somewhat of a problem for scholars, and there is no unanimity as to its meaning. Generally, however, it has been understood as meaning "to cover" or "to wipe off."

One of the purposes of the ancient sacrificial system—in fact, the chief purpose—was to provide atonement, and *kaphar* is used again and again in conjunction with the *daily* sacrificial ritual in Israel. We observe this phenomenon through Leviticus 4, 5, 6, 7, and 8—a phenomenon that (apparently) totally escaped Uriah Smith. As we noted above, atonement for him occurred only once a year—within the sanctuary.

According to the above references, however, *atonement occurred every day* in the courtyard, and that courtyard symbolized this earth on which the cross was planted. This earth, in other words (as we saw in an earlier chapter),[13] is the outer court of the heavenly sanctuary, and Calvary was the altar of burnt offering, where Christ, our Passover, was sacrificed for us.

Despite the fact that atonement happened every day of the year, nevertheless, one special day a year was regarded as "the Day of Atonement"—Yom Kippur (Lev. 23:27; cf. Lev. 16).

When we turn to the New Testament, we are surprised initially to discover that the word "atonement," as such, does not appear at all in most versions. This may come as a shock to the authors of the open letter, who exhibit such a high degree of dogmatism with regard to atonement in the New Testament.

The *concept* of atonement, however, is a cardinal theme—if not *the* cardinal theme—of the New Testament. And the central focus is Jesus Christ—His incarnation and death and no longer the Temple and its rituals. Even so, the sacrificial model features prominently in the wide range of models used to describe the atonement wrought by Jesus Christ, and thought forms drawn from the ancient ritual system are not infrequent.

The biblical picture of atonement is neither simple nor uniform, but very complex and multifaceted. Nor have two millenniums of Christian reflection improved the situation any.

THE ATONEMENT IN CHRISTIAN THOUGHT

Theologians across the centuries have come up with one theory after another in their attempt to articulate the meaning of the saving work of God in Jesus Christ. In order to minimize the confusion of studying a long list of separate theories, I will subsume them, following the style of theologian James Atkinson,[14] under four headings.

1. The Classic or Dramatic Theory—Associated with the early Church Fathers, this theory, as the second part of the name suggests, conceived the atonement in terms of drama. The picture here is that of a great cosmic battle between Christ and the devil—a supernatural struggle that came to a head at Calvary, with Christ emerging victorious.

This theory was adopted and championed by some of the Reformers in the sixteenth century, particularly Martin Luther. According to Atkinson, "the vigour and vitality of Luther's theology spring from this buoyant sense of being on the winning side."[15]

Is there any validity to this particular conception of the atonement? Yes, it has solid New Testament support; and Adventists, after discarding its more esoteric elements—which I will not get into here, may freely endorse its fundamental affirmation. But does it encompass the whole parameter of the atonement? Certainly not.

2. The Juridical (or Satisfaction) Theory—Somewhere in the eleventh century or early part of the twelfth, Anselm, who served for several years as archbishop of Canterbury, wrote a book entitled *Cur Deus Homo* (*Why God Became Man*). In this work he developed a position on the atonement that we know today as the juridical theory. Simply put, it suggests that our defiance of the divine law and government has outraged the majesty of God. Jesus came, therefore, to make amends for us, to offer *satisfaction* in our behalf for the outrage of God's honor. He did this by paying a ransom to God.

Perhaps of all the positions put forward on the atonement, this theory has the most objectionable features—among them, the idea of an offended God needing to be reconciled to us. This notion certainly contradicts the beautiful sentiments of 2 Corinthians 5:19 that "God was in Christ reconciling the world to Himself, not counting their trespasses against them" (NASB).

But even here, as Atkinson observes, the notion of substitution embedded in this view is a valid way of conceiving the atonement, highlighting, as it does, God's immeasurable love in taking the place of sinners and suffering the penalty of sin in their stead. Thus the theory helps to preserve the mercy and the justice of God.

3. The Exemplarist Theory—In the twelfth century a philosopher-theologian named Peter Abelard came up with what we know today as the exemplarist theory of the atonement. According to Abelard, Jesus suffered as the supreme example of God's love and forgiveness. As we behold this astounding demonstration, we are stirred to repentance, which in turn leads to reconciliation with God. This, in Abelard's view, was what the atonement was all about.

Does this find support in Scripture? It does. The New Testament is full of it. But does it encompass the whole parameter of the atonement? Obviously, it does not.

I have noticed, however, that a few of our Adventist theologians attempt to combine a modified version of the exemplarist theory with our own Adventist conception of the great controversy. They seem to consider that position the sum total of what the atonement is about. In other words, they see the death of Christ simply as a *revelation* of God's love—a love that Satan has called into question. According to this view, Christ's death has nothing (or little) to do with substitution or with paying the penalty for sin.

I believe that we need this focus on Christ's death as a revelation of God's love. It is an emphasis that must not die. But to present it as the sum total of what the atonement is about is, in my judgment, a mistake. It succumbs once again to the age-old problem we are discussing just now—the problem of mistaking a part for the whole.

4. The Sacrificial Theory—This theory is associated with no particular person. It is "the only theory to have a systematic exposition in the New Testament, namely in Hebrews. It presents Christ as the priest victim who voluntarily offers up His life in utter obedience to the Father, thereby providing for us an all-sufficient sacrifice. His blood applied to our sinful lives cleanses us and brings us into a state of peace with God." [16]

I find the following assessment of this fourth theory very significant and to the point: "Reflection will show how much theology is held in this one view, how many objections validly met. It delivers us from any subjective view and maintains the objective view of Christ doing what we could never do. It saves from the danger of substitutionary language. It symbolizes in dramatic, historic type how his sprinkled blood restores us to a communion with God wherein we follow the Author, Pioneer, and Finisher of our Faith, *the heavenly high priest active now in our behalf.*" [17]

What have we learned from this historical survey? None of these theories by itself can ever fully comprehend the full scope of God's redemptive work in Christ. From the first century of the Christian Era its vast parameters have ever challenged the keenest theological, philosophical minds within the Christian church.

We have developed creeds on the church, on the Trinity, and

on the Incarnation—to name only three. But the Christian church has never been able to formulate a universal creed on the doctrine of the atonement. The historic theories of the atonement, spread out across the centuries, stand as monuments of the continuing theological struggle to comprehend the full dimension of God's cosmic, saving activity in Jesus Christ.

Accordingly, "no one theory should be . . . seen as antagonistic to another." Each one brings out an important element of the reality in its own unique way. Each is an extended metaphor—helpful for its power to reveal and explain. But each can also conceal—even distort. Nor is the explanatory power of each metaphor constant through history. A particular metaphor (of the atonement, for example) may not necessarily have today the same power and cogency it once held.[18] And even this may be providential.

Our approach, then, ought to be that of drawing out the authentic segments of each theory, "knowing that no one theory, nor any combination of them all, is sufficient to contain the fullness of the reality."[19]

UNDERSTANDING THE ADVENTIST POSITION

In the light of the foregoing, it is somewhat ludicrous to suggest that the Adventist position on the atonement flies in the face of the New Testament teaching on the subject—as if there were any unanimity in the Christian church as to what the New Testament teaches on the question. The fact of the matter is that "no precise explanation . . . is offered in the New Testament, nor has the [Christian] church officially sponsored any one of the theories of the atonement."[20]

So, then, the contribution of Seventh-day Adventists to the ongoing investigation of the atonement has been to focus and elaborate on the sacrificial concept of atonement, interpreting it in the light of the Old Testament sanctuary typology. This approach has led us to broaden the commonly accepted parameters of the atonement. We understand the concept to include not only the sacrifice on the cross but also Christ's work as our high priest in the heavenly sanctuary—including, in particular, that special phase of His ministry which commenced in 1844. (See diagram, p. 56.)

DUALITY OF USAGE

Those who find this dual conception of atonement somewhat troubling may not have noticed that there is indeed a duality inherent in the usage of the word itself.

The Interpreter's Dictionary of the Bible, to name just one source, notes that the English term *atone* was derived from the common phrase "at one." To be "at one" with someone is to be in a state of harmony or agreement. Thus as the word came into our English vocabulary it meant "at onement" or reconciliation. We must ever keep in mind that this definition conceived of atonement as a *state.*[21]

Today this original meaning has been modified, and atonement has come to have a more restricted meaning. It is now generally used to describe the *process* by which the hindrances to reconciliation are removed, rather than the *end* or *state* achieved by their removal, as was the case in the original meaning of the term.[22]

This is an extremely important modern nuance, which we must be careful to keep in mind to avoid misunderstanding atonement terminology. In their use of the term, Adventists include both the original or literal meaning *and also* the more restricted modern meaning of the term.

Thus when Adventists (Ellen G. White included) say that atonement was finished at the cross, they are adopting the more modern use of the word. With the rest of the Protestant world, they mean that the great cosmic transaction that removed the hindrances to reconciliation—the supreme sacrifice of the cross—is finished forever, no more to be repeated.

I, for one, am thoroughly satisfied that in authentic Adventism there is no belittling of the cross whatsoever. The Adventist position leaves the cross precisely where it belongs—at the center. It emphasizes again and again—to anyone willing to listen—that the entire basis of Christ's present high priestly ministry in the heavenly sanctuary is the redemption wrought out on the cross, where Christ offered Himself once for all.

At the forefront of this emphasis was Ellen G. White herself. If anyone is not satisfied with the vigor and depth of her statements on this point, then nothing will satisfy him or her. "The sacrifice of Christ as an atonement for sin is the great truth around which all other truths cluster. In order to be rightly understood and appreciated, every truth in the word of God, from Genesis to Revelation, must be studied in the light that streams from the cross of Calvary. I present before you the great, grand monument of mercy and regeneration, salvation and redemption—the Son of God uplifted on the cross. This is to be the foundation of every discourse given by our ministers." [23]

"Hanging upon the cross Christ was the gospel. . . . This is our message, our argument, our doctrine, our warning to the impenitent, our encouragement for the sorrowing, the hope for every believer. If we can awaken an interest in men's minds that will cause them to fix their eyes on Christ, we may step aside, and ask them only to continue to fix their eyes upon the Lamb of God." [24]

The great atonement hymn by Elisha Hoffman is in the official church hymnal of the Seventh-day Adventist Church, has been there for at least 45 years, and we sing it still today:

> Christ has for sin atonement made,
> What a wonderful Savior!
> We are redeemed!
> The price is paid!
> What a wonderful Savior! [25]

So when Adventists speak of a final atonement transpiring in the heavenly sanctuary, they should be understood in the context of the original meaning of the English word "atonement" described earlier — an activity leading to a *state* of at-one-ment. They imply no belittling of the centrality of the cross. Rather, they mean to suggest that the cross reaches beyond Calvary, beyond A.D. 31 — into the heavenly sanctuary itself, the seat of God's government, the nerve center of human salvation, where Jesus Christ has entered for us within the veil, having been made High Priest forever after the order of Melchizedek.

The *Dictionary of Christian Theology* perceived this eschatological dimension of the atonement: "The doctrine of the atonement is one element in the whole Christian doctrine of salvation which embraces not simply the theological exposition of God's redeeming action in Jesus Christ, which is strictly speaking the doctrine of atonement, but an eschatology which includes judgment and resurrection." [26]

And on this question also, a statement by the respected Reformed theologian L. Berkhof is to the point: "The great and central part of the priestly work of Christ lies in the atonement, but this, of course, is not complete without the intercession. His sacrificial work on earth calls for His service in the heavenly sanctuary. The two are complementary parts of the priestly task of the Saviour." [27]

A WIDER DIMENSION

The wider conception of the atonement that Adventists teach derives from our understanding of the ancient typical system. In line with most Protestants we affirm without hesitation that the entire cultic system, the entire typical system connected with the ancient tabernacle, pointed forward to our Lord's life and death and as such met its fulfillment in the cross. There should be no room for prevarication here, no room for hedging on this point, no room for any awkward stammerings. *Yes, they were fulfilled at the cross!*

However, as we look back at the ancient services on the Day of Atonement, we are able to identify certain important symbolic details associated with Yom Kippur that did not meet complete fulfillment at the cross.

Take, for example, the solemn preparation of the nation of Israel in anticipation of that observance, as we find it described in Leviticus 23:26-29: "And the Lord said to Moses, 'On the tenth day of this seventh month is the day of atonement; it shall be for you a time of holy convocation, and you shall afflict yourselves and present an offering by fire to the Lord. . . . For whoever is not afflicted on this same day shall be cut off from his people' " (RSV).

Nothing approaching this kind of response among God's people occurred at the cross. On the eve of the cross no one in Israel recognized that the most stupendous event in the history of humanity was about to transpire. Even the 12 disciples utterly failed to comprehend it. There was no beating of the breast, no deep contrition, no afflicting of the soul as we find in preparation for the typical Day of Atonement.

But the concept of a final atonement involving judgment in the heavenly sanctuary allows for the conscious, spiritual participation on the part of God's new covenant Israel, as prefigured in the ancient ritual. It was at the commencement of this time of eschatological judgment that the ancient prophet saw mystic angels flying in the midst of heaven, having the everlasting gospel to preach to them that dwell on earth, and to every nation and kindred and tongue and people saying with a loud voice, "Fear God and give him glory, for the hour of his judgment has come" (Rev. 14:7, RSV). Now is the day of judgment. Now is the antitypical day of atonement. Now is the hour for the beating of the breast. Now is the moment for "the afflicting of the soul." Now is the time to call the attention of the nations to this ominous new development in the heavenly sanctuary.

Take, as a second example, the banishment of the goat for Azazel. Here too there is a sense in which Satan—if we see him as the meaning of that symbolism—was banished at the cross. In John 12:31 Jesus said, shortly before the cross, "Now is the judgment of this world, now shall the ruler of this world be cast out" (RSV). I believe that this was a reference to the banishment of Satan from heaven.

But we would also have to admit that Satan has not been banished in any final sense. Does not the apostle say that the devil like a roaring lion seeks his prey to devour (1 Peter 5:8)? And does not that great voice from heaven pronounce a woe to the inhabitants of the earth because of the coming of Satan (Rev. 12:12)? And who among us has not felt the awful sting of his fiery dart and sensed the need to don the Christian armor against this supernatural contingent "from the very headquarters of evil" (Eph. 6:10-16, Phillips)?

No, the devil has not yet been banished in any ultimate sense. He is still very much around, unfortunately. Only at the end of the millennium shall we see the full eschatological fulfillment of that ancient symbolism enacted in the wilderness tabernacle.

Take, as a third and final example, the cleansing of the sanctuary itself. This was the main focus of Yom Kippur, and some think they see the fulfillment of the symbolism at the cross. In other words, they maintain that the heavenly sanctuary was cleansed at the cross.

Was the heavenly sanctuary cleansed at the cross? Yes, the sanctuary was cleansed at the cross. The cross produced, among other things, a cleansing—in the sense of a clearing—of the name of the heavenly Father, a vindication of His government of love and justice.

But if the cleansing of the sanctuary involves also the final justification of God in the eyes of the universe, to the extent that all cosmic questions are resolved and the entire universe of created intelligences recognizes the integrity of God's government, then no one can successfully contend that this was completely accomplished at the cross. Thousands of bloody wars have bedeviled us since the cross. Hundreds of millions of humans slaughtered in ghastly carnage. Natural disasters, pestilences, famines, and the modern scourge of terrorism and drug abuse have added their share to the deadly toll. A million "whys" break the silence of each day. A million tears drench countless pillows at the midnight hour. A huge question mark still lingers unerased in the cosmic sky, indicative to any sensitive observer that ultimate atonement is not yet here.

This came vividly to me many years ago when I was a young student literature evangelist. I was canvassing in the little town of Vanderhoof, British Columbia. I entered a home that morning and spread out my demonstration sheet on the floor. About three minutes into the canvass I became aware that I was speaking into the wind. I looked up to find the object of my presentation gazing across at me with pensive, angry eyes. Bewildered, I sought the reason for her militant grief. She told me her story.

A few months before my visit, her husband was loading grain onto a truck. Suddenly the entire load capsized and rammed him to his death. About a month or two later her brother, a construction worker in the city of Prince George, about 60 miles away, touched a high-tension wire and was electrocuted immediately. (I happened to know about the incident since I had just arrived from canvassing in Prince George.)

She mentioned one more detail: "My daughter, who lived in Alberta at the time, was flying over with her husband for the funeral of her brother. They went down with the plane that crashed near Cache Creek." She did not have to explain. I had also read in the papers about the crash (about 300 miles to the south). I knew that everyone on board had been killed.

All this tragedy had come to her within a period of six months. Her husband, her brother, her daughter, her son-in-law — all dead. "If there is a God," she said in frigid anger, "He's a wicked God."

At this point I folded my demonstration spread and for the next half hour attempted to bring some solace to that grieving heart and to paint a better picture of my God.

Millions of people the world over share that Vanderhoof lady's gruesome picture of the God we serve. Richard Rubenstein, one of the "God is dead" theologians of the 1960s, spoke for all of them as he reflected on the Nazi atrocities of the 1940s, which saw the massacre of millions of Jews. Said Rubenstein: "We stand in a cold, silent, unfeeling cosmos. . . . After Auschwitz, what else can a Jew say about God?" [28]

No, the questions have not all been answered yet. The integrity of God's sanctuary and government is not yet clear to all. The cosmic culprit is still at large. The sanctuary, in other words, is not yet fully cleansed, not yet fully *justified*, not yet fully *vindicated*. Thus, the atonement, in the sense of "at-onement," has not yet been accomplished.

None of us can adequately explain why it's taking so long. We might argue that a computer, given the right kind of data, could judge all humanity in much less time than 150 years—the period since 1844. But in the first place, God does not react to time as humans do. Second Peter 3:8 makes it clear that the passage of time, as we experience it, means little to God.

In the second place, God, unlike a computer, is not dealing mechanically with numbers, statistics, and theoretical data. He is dealing with people—precious beings He has created—and with their eternal destiny. We are important to Him, and He is taking His time. "The Lord is not slow about His promise, as some count slowness, but is patient toward you, not wishing for any to perish but for all to come to repentance" (2 Peter 3:9, NASB).

WHEN ATONEMENT IS COMPLETE

But Scripture is explicit about how it all will end, how God will put it all together and make things whole again. As the final process starts, "the Lord himself shall descend from heaven with a shout, with the voice of the archangel, and with the trump of God: and the dead in Christ shall rise first: then we which are alive and remain shall be caught up together with them in the clouds, to meet the Lord in the air: and so shall we ever be with the Lord" (1 Thess. 4:16, 17).

With the coming of atonement, great cosmic jubilee trumpets will sound throughout the universe (1 Cor. 15:52). "The dead will be raised imperishable, and we shall be changed" (verse 52, RSV). "For this corruptible must put on incorruption, and this mortal must put on immortality. So when this corruptible shall have put on incorruption, and this mortal shall have put on immortality, then shall be brought to pass the saying that is written, Death is swallowed up in victory" (verses 53, 54).

Then that mother who was forced to place her precious little bundle under the cold sod, that poor child left orphaned by the cruel hand of death, husbands and wives left alone and grieving by that grim reaper—they shall all sing then, they shall all laugh then, they shall all join in a universal taunt: "O death, where is thy sting? O grave, where is thy victory?" (verse 55).

With the coming of at-onement, there will be "new heavens and a new earth, wherein dwelleth righteousness," for the people who live there will "do justly," and "love mercy," and "walk humbly" with their God (2 Peter 3:13; Micah 6:8). And God will bring to justice all the criminals of the earth, all the perpetrators of atrocities against humanity, all the oppressors and miscreants of the centuries. And a great voice will shout from the heavenly temple: "Yea, Lord God, the Almighty, true and just are thy judgments!" (Rev. 16:7, RSV).

There will be no more international rivalry, bitterness, and war—for all the tyrants who fostered them will be gone. No more racial conflicts—for all the bigots who incited them will be gone. No more racial prejudices—for those who harbored them will be gone.

There will be no more crime, no more substance abuse, no more murder, no more sexual perversion or immorality, no more corruption. For "there shall in no wise enter into it any thing that defileth, neither whatsoever worketh abomination, or maketh a lie: but they which are written in the Lamb's book of life" (Rev. 21:27). There will be "new heavens and a new earth, in which righteousness dwells" (2 Peter 3:13, NASB).

And there will be no more sickness, no more pain, no more death. "For the former things are passed away" (Rev. 21:4). The people "shall not say, I am sick," for those who dwell there "shall be forgiven their iniquity" (Isa. 33:24). And the "ransomed of the Lord shall return, and come to Zion with songs and everlasting joy upon their heads: they shall obtain joy and gladness, and sorrow and sighing shall flee away" (Isa. 35:10).

That's it, friends. That's it — at last!

"The great controversy is ended. Sin and sinners are no more. The entire universe is clean. One pulse of harmony and gladness beats through the vast creation. From Him who created all flow life and light and gladness throughout the realms of illimitable space. From the minutest atom to the greatest world, all things, animate and inanimate, in their unshadowed beauty and perfect joy, declare that God is love." [29]

Does this sound like something that flies in the face of the gospel? Does this sound like a prostitution of righteousness by faith? No, this is the most beautiful thing I've come across in all my sampling of theology and philosophy. Thank God for the great transaction at the cross once for all enacted. Thank God for the great high-priestly ministry of Jesus in the heavenly sanctuary. Thank God for the blessed hope! Thank God for this wonderful future! With all my soul I want to say, "Thanks be to God!"

---

[1] "An Open Letter to CLM [Central Luzon Mission] President Avelino Canlas," May 19, 1981. (In my personal files.)

[2] Ibid.

[3] Uriah Smith, The Sanctuary and the 2300 Days of Daniel 8:14 (Battle Creek, Mich.: SDA Pub. Assn., 1877), p. 276.

[4] See Adams, The Sanctuary Doctrine, pp. 58-62.

[5] Ellen G. White, The Great Controversy (Mountain View, Calif.: Pacific Press Pub. Assn., 1911), p. 489.

[6] Ibid., p. 421.

[7] _____ , in Signs of the Times, Aug. 16, 1899. In Questions on Doctrines (Washington, D.C.: Review and Herald Pub. Assn., 1957), p. 664.

[8] Ibid. (Italics supplied.)

[9] Ibid., June 28, 1899. (Italics supplied.) In Questions on Doctrines, p. 663.

[10] _____ , The Desire of Ages (Mountain View, Calif.: Pacific Press Pub. Assn., 1898), p. 819. (Italics supplied.)

[11] _____ , in *Review and Herald*, Sept. 24, 1901. (Italics supplied.) In *Questions on Doctrine*, p. 663.

[12] I am indebted to the *Interpreter's Dictionary of the Bible*, vol. A-D, pp. 309-313 for some of the material in this section.

[13] See chapter 4.

[14] In *A Dictionary of Christian Theology*, ed. Alan Richardson (Philadelphia: Westminster Press, 1969), s.v. "Atonement." (For an insightful and engaging assessment of the doctrine of the atonement, see G. Aulen, *Christus Victor*.)

[15] *Dictionary of Christian Theology*, p. 23.

[16] *Ibid.*

[17] *Ibid.*, p. 24. (Italics supplied.)

[18] I am indebted to Richard W. Coffen for this insight.

[19] Aulen, *Christus Victor*, p. 22.

[20] *Interpreter's Dictionary of the Bible*, vol. A-D, p. 313.

[21] *Ibid.*, p. 309.

[22] *Ibid.*

[23] Ellen G. White, *Gospel Workers* (Washington, D.C.: Review and Herald Pub. Assn., 1948), p. 315.

[24] Ellen G. White, manuscript 49, 1898. In *Questions on Doctrine*, p. 662.

[25] *The SDA Hymnal*, No. 335. Cf. *The Church Hymnal: Official Hymnal of the Seventh-day Adventist Church* (Washington, D.C.: Review and Herald Pub. Assn., 1941), No. 644.

[26] *Dictionary of Christian Theology*, s.v., "Atonement."

[27] L. Berkhof, *Systematic Theology*, 4th revised and enlarged ed. (Grand Rapids: Wm. B. Eerdmans Pub. Co., 1939, 1941), p. 367.

[28] Richard Rubenstein, *After Auschwitz* (Indianapolis: Bobbs-Merrill Co., 1966), p. 152.

[29] *The Great Controversy*, p. 678.

A Testimony

(Written in 1981, this testimony—in modified form—first appeared in the *Adventist Review*, Nov. 4, 1982, pp. 7, 8. I include it here so that readers may have a better understanding of where I'm coming from, as they say, and my approach to the subject covered in this book.)

When I embarked on graduate study in the mid-1960s, I became aware of certain misgivings among Adventists over the doctrine of the sanctuary. Some people seemed to regard it as a kind of skeleton in the Adventist closet.

Because of the central place of the doctrine in the Adventist Church, this attitude gave me a deep sense of uneasiness. I had been reared in the Anglican Church and left its communion when I could no longer square its teachings with the Scriptures. Was I to face the same situation in my adopted church? The matter was laid to rest as soon as I left the academic circles of the university for the pastoral ministry.

Several years later, however, I was back in academia, facing the prospect of writing a doctoral dissertation. I chose to work on the Seventh-day Adventist doctrine of the sanctuary. But how was I to proceed?

At the secondary school I attended as a teenager, the spirit of dispassionate investigation and research was fostered. We were encouraged to examine critically the validity of every assertion, regardless of its source. This deeply ingrained attitude I was to bring to a subject regarded by many Adventists as the most precarious doctrine we hold.

It was, therefore, with no little trepidation that I began my work, leaning heavily on the security provided by a university setting. An examination of the existing literature showed that no one before me had undertaken such an approach to the doctrine, and I often felt like the proverbial fool rushing in where angels fear to tread. My only consolation (if also frustration) was that mine was not a rushing but rather a slow, painstaking examination of the subject. I was encouraged by statements from Ellen G. White's writings to the effect that truth can bear investigation, and that every doctrine we hold must be critically examined by *us*. [1]

This was all the guidance I allowed myself to have from the writings of Ellen G. White, however. Being fully aware of the criticism that Adventists base their sanctuary doctrine on her writings, I considered it highly improper to give those writings any normative value in my assessment of the sanctuary teaching. Thus I deliberately attempted, throughout my dissertation, to create a mental block as to what Mrs. White had said on the subject.

This approach might be questioned by some well-meaning loyalists within the church. However, if Adventists refuse to subject the teaching of the fathers to the acid test of Scripture and reason, but instead blindly cling to tradition, how are they different from Catholic or Mormon traditionalists? We expect those Catholics or Mormons who sit under our preaching to subject the tradition of *their* fathers to critical, unbiased assessment. Do we demand less of ourselves? My approach had to be shaped by thoughts of this kind. I had to forget, as it were, that I was a Seventh-day Adventist, and pursue my research with as little prejudice as humanly possible.

It is precisely at this critical point, however, that many researchers err. They assume an "anti" instead of a "neutral" stance. It is all too easy for an Adventist scholar, in order to appear objective, to actually adopt, sometimes unconsciously, an anti-Adventist attitude, something regarded as chic in some circles. But this is a betrayal of the very objectivity so necessary to the scholarly enterprise because of its potential to deceive both the researcher and the reader.

In their attempts to arrive at a point of as complete neutrality as possible, scholars, moreover, must examine their inner motivations. It is easy for negative experiences or unworthy motives of one kind or another to translate into a jaundiced, one-sided approach to a particular problem. For example, the last bad sermon on a particular theme, the anger or resentment nursed for some administrator or colleague, the penchant to conform to generally accepted theological norms in the Protestant world, the desire to be considered loyalist by denominational leaders, the urge to achieve notoriety or to be regarded as avant-garde—or any other of a score of egocentric factors. Any one of these may help to skew scholarly thinking or conclusions. It is a very precarious business.

Constantly reminding myself of the pitfalls, I labored week after weary week on the topic. In addition to comparing the position of the church with Scripture, I read every critique of the Adventist position I could find up to and including the early part of August 1980, when my work ended. My investigation commenced before the recent unrest within the church over the question of the sanctuary and was therefore not precipitated by it. However, that debate served to heighten the significance of my study, giving me the assurance that the work which engaged so many of my waking hours was far from purely academic.

When the debate broke into the open sometime in the fall of 1979, I was approached almost daily by some who knew the area of my research for my opinion on one issue or another in relation to the sanctuary doctrine. But for more than six months I simply refused to comment substantially, while I struggled with the issues in my own mind.

As I waded deeper and deeper into the subject, I was frankly nervous as to where my research might lead. My commitment to the task of impassioned, unprejudiced research, strengthened by my dissertation committee, frightened me. What if my findings and conclusions proved inimical to the fundamental teachings of the Adventist Church on this question? It was not that I thought my conclusions would, necessarily, invalidate the church's position—I was not that arrogant. My concern was rather for myself, for my personal relationship to the church in the event I should come to the conclusion that on such a fundamental tenet of its faith, it was in error.

After nearly two years of critical appraisal, I was ready to write my conclusions. I criticized, sometimes rather strongly, the position that certain prominent Adventist theologians (and the church as a whole) have taken in the past, and called attention to positive contributions to the doctrine of the sanctuary made by some of the church's critics, notably Albion Fox Ballenger. This same dispassionate investigation led, however, to the conclusion that "no evidence to which [my] study had access was considered fatal to any fundamental area of [the doctrine of the sanctuary] as developed by Seventh-day Adventists."[2]

The weight of this conclusion must not be underestimated. It means to say that I have seen *no persuasive evidence* that invalidates our basic teachings in regard to the significance of 1844, or a pre-Advent judgment, or a final atonement centered in the heavenly sanctuary with the cross as its focus. I believe that these positions are not only theologically sound but also philosophically exciting.

Less than 72 hours after writing the conclusions to my dissertation, I was sitting as a delegate to the Glacier View (Colorado) conference on the sanctuary. Notwithstanding the purpose for which we had assembled, my own private agenda was to observe whether the conclusions I had just written would need to be revamped or even abandoned in the wake of the findings of the conference. To my great relief, especially since my work had not yet been defended, the deliberations left my conclusions regarding the soundness of the church's basic positions on the sanctuary intact.

Furthermore, I came away with my faith in the integrity of the sanctuary doctrine greatly strengthened. For day after day at the conference I had witnessed what I considered to be free and frank discussions on the important issues surrounding this topic by some of the keenest theological minds in the denomination. The consensus that resulted has been a profound inspiration to me. It is a dimension that my lonely study in a carrel at Andrews University could not have supplied.

This appendix does not attempt to present the arguments that led me to the conclusions I describe.[3] It cannot detail the biblical, rational, or suprarational considerations that brought conviction to me, even on the deeper levels of consciousness. It is rather a simple testimony of how one student of the sanctuary doctrine has settled for himself an issue of current theological concern within the Adventist Church.

[1] See Ellen G. White, *Counsels to Writers and Editors*, p. 35; *Testimonies* (Mountain View, Calif.: Pacific Press Pub. Assn., 1948), vol. 5, pp. 707, 708.

[2] See Adams, *The Sanctuary Doctrine*, p. 283.

[3] Those who wish to follow my reasoning may consult my dissertation, referred to in note 2.

Index

CPSIA information can be obtained at www.ICGtesting.com
Printed in the USA
BVOW021701040313

314473BV00005B/10/P